VOL 02

AIR FRYER COOKBOOK

FOR BEGINNERS

1001 QUICK & EASY
FOOLPROOF RECIPES,
THE CREATIVE GUIDE
TO USE THE **AIR FRYER**
IN THE BEST
AND HEALTHY WAY

What's Inside

Introduction

The multi-functional Air Fryer is made to start your adventure in cooking.

To do so successfully, though, you must begin to learn all the functions and options that this great kitchen helper has.

Yes, it is exciting, and we all want to rush off and start cooking and baking, which is excellent. Staring at the results of flopped recipes is not so great, though. See what you may need to buy extra and take to heart the tips from people who learned the hard way to do and what not to do

The Different Cooking Modes

People often ask why the Air Fryer has so many different cooking modes when the different ways of basics functions are the same. The reason for this is that the Vortex uses smart programming to assist you in air frying, baking, etcetera at the optimal temperatures and best pre-selected times. The programming is intuitive and guides you along through the whole cooking process. It tells you when to add the food, when to rotate the cooking trays, and when to remove it. What makes the Vortex different from stovetop cooking and oven baking is that the Vortex uses rapid air circulation to cook and bake food with minimum oil or no oil.

AIR FRYER

It cooks the foods evenly, both fresh and frozen, with a crisp and crunchy outside while the inside

of the food stays moist and soft.

BAKE

This mode works equally well for cakes, muffins, cupcakes, and delicious baked lasagna. You can bake larger quantities as you have two cooking trays.

ROAST

This function is for more significant cuts of meat that cannot be accommodated on the rotisserie, which is designed to take a maximum weight of 4 lbs. More significant roast pieces are placed on one of the perforated cooking trays, so you achieve the same crisp outside you get for smaller items on the rotisserie.

ROTISSERIE

You can use the rotisserie basket and the rotisserie spit, depending on what you want to cook.

Smaller items can go into the basket and bigger roasts on the spit. You get an all-over crisply browned outside, a succulent inside, and all the fats drip out onto the drip pan at the bottom of the oven.

BROIL

Broiling is done by placing the food on a cooking tray in the highest rack slot.

This is for fast cooking with intense heat for short periods. The perforated cooking tray allows fats and liquids to drip out, making the food much less greasy.

REHEATING

Fast reheating option for single portions of food and more massive amounts and warms the food evenly.

DEHYDRATE

Dehydration is a slow process, and as with any dehydration, you have to be patient. The food you dehydrate in the Vortex stays flavorful throughout the whole process.

BENEFITS OF THE AIR FRYER SMART PROGRAMMING

The Vortex comes pre-programmed with ten smart programs for each of the different cooking modes. This includes default temperatures and cooking times for each of the cooking modes. This makes it very easy to use this multi-functional appliance

as it takes the guesswork out of which cooking mode to use and what the optimal temperature for any specific cooking mode is.

The programming also tells you when to place the food inside the air fryer, when to turn food over or rotate the cooking trays, and when to remove the food from the air fryer

INCREDIBLY VERSATILE

There is currently no other appliance on the market that incorporates seven different cooking modes in one device. You would need several various machines for the same functions that the Vortex offers.

CONVENIENCE

You do not have to go out to get fast food; you can make a healthier option at home. The rotisserie presents you with a crisp whole chicken and roast meat without a stove oven. You can switch instantly between cooking different types of food; there is no need to invest in several appliances.

COOKS FAST

The Vortex cooks faster, so you can have deep-fried tasting food much quicker than conventional deep-frying.

TABLE OF CONTENTS

Chapter-1: 25 Special Recipes

Chapter-2: Breakfast Recipes

Chapter-3: Lunch Recipes

Chapter-4: Dinner Recipes

Chapter-5: Snack Recipes

Vegetable Quiche

INTERMEDIATE RECIPE

NUTRITION

Calories 255 Fat 16 g Carbohydrates 8 g, Sugar 4.2 g
Protein 21 g Cholesterol 257 mg

6

SHOPPING LIST

- 8 eggs
- 1 cup of coconut milk
- 1 cup tomatoes, chopped & 1 of zucchini
- 1 tablespoon butter
- 1 onion, chopped
- 1 cup Parmesan cheese, grated
- 1/2 teaspoon pepper
- 1 teaspoon salt

DIRECTIONS

10 MINUTES

24 MINUTES

1. Preheat the air fryer to 370°F.
2. Melt butter in a pan over medium heat then add onion and
3. sauté until onion lightly brown.
4. Add tomatoes and zucchini to the pan and
5. sauté for 4-5 minutes.
6. Transfer cooked vegetables into the air fryer baking dish.
7. Beat eggs with cheese, milk, pepper, and salt in a bowl.
8. Pour egg mixture over vegetables in a baking dish.
9. Place dish in the air fryer and cook for 24 minutes or until eggs are set.
10. Slice and serve.

10 MINUTES

10 MINUTES

1

Scallion Sandwich

BASIC RECIPES

SHOPPING LIST

- 2 slices of wheat bread
- 2 teaspoons butter, low fat
- 2 scallions, sliced thinly
- 1 tablespoon of parmesan cheese, grated
- 3/4 cup of cheddar cheese, reduced-fat,
- grated

NUTRITION

Calorie: 154 Carbs 9g
Fat 2.5g Protein 8.6g Fiber 2.4g

DIRECTIONS

1. Preheat the Air fryer to 356°F
2. Spread butter on a slice of bread.
3. Place inside cooking basket butter side down.
4. Top with cheese and scallions.
5. Spread the rest of the butter on the other slice of bread
6. Put it on top of the sandwich
7. Sprinkle with parmesan cheese.
8. Cook for 10 minutes.

Lean Lamb and Turkey Meatballs with Yogurt

INTERMEDIATE RECIPE

NUTRITION

Calorie: 154 Carbs 9g
Fat 2.5g Protein 8.6g Fiber 2.4g

SHOPPING LIST

- 1 egg white
- 4 ounces ground lean turkey
- 1 pound of ground lean lamb
- 1 teaspoon each of cayenne pepper, ground
- coriander, red chili paste, salt, and ground
- cumin
- 2 garlic cloves, minced
- 1 1/2 tablespoons parsley, chopped
- 1 tablespoon mint, chopped
- 1/4 cup of olive oil
For the yogurt
- 2 tablespoons of buttermilk
- 1 garlic clove, minced
- 1/4 cup mint, chopped
- 1/2 cup of Greek yogurt, non-fat
- Salt to taste

DIRECTIONS

1. Set the Air Fryer to 390°F.
2. Mix all the ingredients for the meatballs in a bowl.
3. Roll and mold them into golf-size round pieces.
4. Place in the cooking basket.
5. Cook for 8 minutes. While you wait, combine all the ingredients for the mint yogurt in a bowl. Mix well. Serve the meatballs with mint yogurt. Top with olives and fresh mint.

Spinach & Mozzarella Muffins

INTERMEDIATE RECIPE

NUTRITION

Calories 251
Total Fat 16.7 g Saturated Fat 8.6 g
Cholesterol 222 mg Sodium 495 mg
Total Carbs 3.1 g Fiber 0 g
Sugar 0.4 g
Protein 22.8 g

SHOPPING LIST

- 2 large eggs
- 2 tablespoons half-and-half
- 2 tablespoons frozen spinach, thawed
- 4 teaspoons mozzarella cheese, grated
- Salt and ground black pepper, as required

DIRECTIONS

1. Grease 2 ramekins. In each prepared ramekin, break 1 egg.
2. Divide the half and half, spinach, cheese, salt and black pepper, and each ramekin and stir gently to mix.
3. combine, without breaking the yolks.
4. Press "Power Button" of Air Fry and turn the dial to select the "Air Fry" mode.
5. Press the Time button and turn the dial again to set the cook time to 10 minutes.
6. Now push the Temp button and rotate the dial to set the temperature at 330°F.
7. Press the "Start/Pause" button to start. When the unit beeps to show that it is preheated, open the lid.
8. Arrange the ramekins over the "Wire Rack" and insert them in the oven.
9. Serve warm.

10 MINUTES

10 MINUTES

2

Potato & Bell Pepper Hash

INTERMEDIATE RECIPE

SHOPPING LIST

- 2 cups of water
- 5 russet potatoes, peeled and cubed
- ½ tablespoon extra-virgin olive oil
- ½ of onion, chopped
- ½ of jalapeño, chopped
- 1 green bell pepper, seeded and chopped
- ¼ teaspoon dried oregano, crushed
- ¼ teaspoon garlic powder
- ¼ teaspoon ground cumin
- ¼ teaspoon red chili powder
- Salt and freshly ground black pepper, as
- needed

NUTRITION

Calories 251
Total Fat 16.7 g Saturated Fat 8.6 g
Cholesterol 222 mg Sodium 495 mg
Total Carbs 3.1 g Fiber 0 g
Sugar 0.4 g
Protein 22.8 g

15 MINUTES

DIRECTIONS

1. In a large bowl, add the water and potatoes and steep for about 30 minutes.
2. Drain well and pat dry with the paper towels. In a bowl, add the potatoes and oil and toss to coat well.
3. Press "Power Button" of Air Fry and turn the dial to select the "Air Fry" mode. Press the Time button and again turn the dial to set the cook time to 5 minutes.
4. Now push the Temp button and rotate the dial to set the temperature at 330°F.
5. Press the "Start/Pause" button to start. When the unit beeps to indicate that it is preheated, open the lid.
6. Arrange the potato cubes in "Air Fry Basket" and insert them in the oven.
7. Transfer the potatoes to a plate. In a bowl, add the potatoes and remaining ingredients and toss to coat well. Press "Power Button" of Air Fryer and turn the dial to select the "Air Fry" mode.
8. Press the Time button and turn the dial again to set the cooking.

time to 20 minutes. Now push the Temp button and turn the dial to set the temperature at 390^0F.

9. Press the "Start/Pause" button to start. When the unit beeps to indicate that it is preheated, open the lid.

10. Arrange the vegetable mixture in "Air Fry Basket" and insert it in the oven. Serve hot.

25 MINUTES

4

Peri Peri Roasted Chicken

INTERMEDIATE RECIPE

SHOPPING LIST

- ½ cup olive oil
- 1/3 cup BBQ sauce
- 3 tbsp Worcestershire sauce
- 2 tbsp freshly minced garlic
- 1 tbsp onion powder
- ½ lemon, juiced
- 3 tbsp hot sauce
- 1 tsp yellow mustard
- Salt and black pepper to taste
- 1 (3 lbs.) whole chicken

DIRECTIONS

1. Insert the drip tray into the bottom of the air fryer and preheat the device at Roast mode at 400ºF for 2 to 3 minutes.
2. In a small bowl, mix all the ingredients up to the chicken. Pat the chicken dry with paper towels and with gloves on your hands.
3. Rub the marinade all around and inside the cavity of the chicken.
4. Use cooking twines to tie and secure the wings, legs, and any loose ends into the body of the chicken.
5. Run the rotisserie spit through one open end of the chicken through to the other end and lock the forks with their screws.
6. Lift the chicken, lock the spit onto the lever in the oven and close the lid.
7. Set the timer to 50 minutes and press Start.
8. Cook until the chicken is golden brown all around and the meat tenders almost falling off the bone.
9. When done cooking, open the oven and use the rotisserie lift to remove the chicken off the lever.
10. Unscrew, pull out the spit, and allow the chicken to sit for 3 to 5 minutes before slicing and serving.

10 MINUTES

25 MINUTES

4

NUTRITION

Calories 452 Total Fat 31.41g
Total Carbs 9.15g Fiber 1.2g
Protein 33.15g Sugar 3.55g
Sodium 506mg

Coffee Spiced Rib Eye Steak

INTERMEDIATE RECIPE

SHOPPING LIST

- 1 tsp brown sugar
- ¼ tsp chipotle powder
- 14 | P a g .
- 1/8 tsp coriander powder
- ¼ tsp paprika
- ½ tsp ground coffee
- ½ tsp black pepper
- ¼ tsp chili powder
- 1/8 tsp cocoa powder
- 1 ½ tsp salt
- ¼ tsp garlic powder
- ¼ tsp onion powder
- 1 lb. ribeye steak

NUTRITION

Calories 218
Total Fat 12.99g
Total Carbs 3.31g
Fiber 0.3g
Protein 22.21g
Sugar 0.66g Sodium 977mg

DIRECTIONS

1. Insert the dripping pan at the bottom of the air fryer and preheat the oven at Roast mode at 390⁰F for 2 to 3 minutes.
2. In a small bowl, mix all the ingredients except for the meat and then, season the meat well and on both sides with the spice mix.
3. Allow sitting at room temperature for 20 minutes to marinate.
4. Next, place the meat on the cooking tray, insert the tray on the middle rack of the oven, and close the device.
5. Set the timer for 9 minutes and press Start.
6. Cook the meat without touching it until the timer reads to the end.
7. When ready, transfer the meat onto a clean, flat surface and allow resting for 5 minutes before slicing.
8. Serve warm afterward.

30 MINUTES

14 MINUTES

4

Greek Style Mini Burger Pies

INTERMEDIATE RECIPE

NUTRITION

Calories 270 Fat 15.0 g

Protein 19.0 g

Carbohydrates 13.0 g

15 MINUTES

DIRECTIONS

1. Preheat the air fryer at 350°F.
2. Grease 12 muffin cups with cooking spray. Cook the onion and beef in a skillet heated on medium-high. Once the beef is browned and cooked through, drain and let cool for five minutes.
3. Stir together with feta cheese, roasted red peppers, and red pepper flakes.
4. Whisk the baking mixture ingredients together.
5. Fill each muffin cup with the baking mixture (1 tablespoon).
6. Air-fry for twenty-five to thirty minutes.
7. Let cool before serving.

40 MINUTES

SHOPPING LIST

- Burger mixture:
- Onion, large, chopped (1 piece)
- Red bell peppers, roasted, diced (1/2 cup)
- Ground lamb, 80% lean (1 pound)
- Red pepper flakes (1/4 teaspoon)
- Feta cheese, crumbled (2 ounces)
- Baking mixture
- Milk (1/2 cup)
- Biscuit mix, classic (1/2 cup)
- Eggs (2 pieces)

6

Family Fun Pizza

INTERMEDIATE RECIPE

SHOPPING LIST

- Pizza crust
- Water, warm (1 cup)
- Salt (1/2 teaspoon)
- Flour, whole wheat (1 cup)
- Olive oil (2 tablespoons)
- Dry yeast, quick active (1 package)
- Flour, all-purpose (1 ½ cups)
- Cornmeal
- Olive oil
- Onion, chopped (1 cup)
- Mushrooms, sliced, drained (4 ounces)
- Garlic cloves, chopped finely (2 pieces)
- Parmesan cheese, grated (1/4 cup)
- Ground lamb, 80% lean (1 pound) Italian seasoning (1 teaspoon)
- Pizza sauce (8 ounces)
- Mozzarella cheese (2 cups)

NUTRITION

Calories 215
Carbohydrates 20.0 g
Fat 10.0 g
Protein 13.0 g

DIRECTIONS

1. Mix yeast with warm water. Combine with flour, oil (2 tablespoons), and salt by stirring and then whisking vigorously for half a minute. Let the dough sit for twenty minutes.
2. Preheat the air fryer at 350°F.
3. Prep 2 square pans (8-inch) by greasing with oil before sprinkling with cornmeal.
4. Cut the rested dough in half; place each half inside each pan. Set aside, covered, for thirty to forty-five minutes.
5. Cook in the deep fryer for twenty to twenty-two minutes.
6. Sauté the onion, beef, garlic, and Italian seasoning until beef is completely cooked.
7. Drain and reserve
8. Cover the air-fried crusts with pizza sauce before topping with beef mixture, cheeses, and mushrooms. Return to the air fryer and cook for twenty minutes. seasoning until beef is completely cooked. Drain and set aside.
9. Cover the air-fried crusts with pizza sauce before topping with beef mixture, cheeses, and mushrooms. Return to the air fryer and cook for twenty minutes.

30 MINUTES

25 MINUTES

16

Tso's Cauliflower

BASIC RECIPE

NUTRITION

Calories 301
Total Fat 12.2g
Saturated Fat 2.4g
Cholesterol 110 mg
Sodium 276 mg
Total Carbs 12.5g
Fiber 0.9g
Sugar 1.4g
Protein 8.8g

SHOPPING LIST

- 1 head cauliflower, cut in florets
- ¾ cup all-purpose flour, divided
- 3 eggs
- 1 cup panko breadcrumbs
- Tso sauce
- Canola or peanut oil
- 2 tbsps.oyster sauce
- ¼ cup soy sauce
- 2 teaspoon chili paste
- 2 tbsps. rice wine vinegar
- 2 table spoons of sugar
- ¼ cup of water

DIRECTIONS

1. Add cauliflower to a large bowl and sprinkle ¼ cup flour over it.
2. Whisk eggs in one bowl, spread panko crumbs in another, and put remaining flour in a third bowl.
3. Dredge the cauliflower florets through the flour then dip in the eggs.
4. Coat them with breadcrumbs.
5. Place the coated cauliflower florets in the air fryer basket and spray them with cooking oil.
6. Return the fryer basket to the air fryer and cook on air fry mode for 15 minutes at 400°F.
7. Prepare the Tso sauce by mixing all its ingredients in a saucepan.
8. Stir and cook this mixture for 10 minutes until it thickens.
9. Pour this sauce over the air fried cauliflower florets.
10. Enjoy.

5 MINUTES

25 MINUTES

2

Lemon Roasted Chicken

BASIC RECIPE

10 MINUTES | 55 MINUTES | 4

DIRECTIONS

1. Insert the drip tray into the bottom of the air fryer and preheat the device at Roast mode at 400⁰F for 2 to 3 minutes.
2. In a small bowl, mix the olive oil, butter, lemon zest, lemon juice, garlic, salt, and black pepper.
3. Pat the chicken dries with paper towels and rub the seasoning mix all around and inside the cavity of the chicken. Use cooking twines to tie and secure the wings, legs, and any loose ends into the body of the chicken. Run the rotisserie spit through one open end of the chicken through to the other end and lock the forks with their screws.
4. Lift the chicken, lock the spit onto the lever in the oven and close the lid. Set the timer to 50 minutes and press Start. Cook until the chicken is golden brown all around and the meat tender almost falling off the bone.
5. When done cooking, open the oven and use the rotisserie lift to remove the chicken off the lever.
6. Unscrew, pull out the spit, and allow the chicken to sit for 3 to 5 minutes before slicing and serving.

SHOPPING LIST

- 2 tbsp olive oil
- 2 tbsp butter, softened
- 1 lemon, zested and juiced
- 4 garlic cloves, minced
- Salt and black pepper to taste
- 1 (3 lbs.) whole chicken

NUTRITION

Calories 296 Total Fat 16.81g
Total Carbs 2.89g
Fiber 0.3g
Protein 32.39 g
Sugar 0.91 g
Sodium 165 mg

Air Fried Tofu with Peanut Dipping Sauce

BASIC RECIPE

DIRECTIONS

1. In a bowl, mix all dipping sauce ingredients.
2. Cover it with plastic wrap and keep refrigerated until ready to serve.
3. To make the fried tofu, season all-purpose flour with salt and pepper.
4. Coat the tofu cubes with the flour mixture.
5. Drizzle with oil.
6. Preheat your Air Fryer to 390°F. Place coated tofu in the cooking basket.
7. Be careful not to overcrowd them.
8. Cook until browned for approximately 8 minutes. Serve with prepared peanut dipping sauce.
9. Enjoy!

NUTRITION

Calories 256

Fat 14.1 g

Carbs 21.2 g

Protein 12.4 g.

5 MINUTES

8 MINUTES

6

SHOPPING LIST

- 16 oz. cubed firm tofu
- 185g all-purpose flour
- ½ teaspoon Himalayan salt
- ½ teaspoon ground black pepper
- Olive oil spray
- For the dipping sauce:
- 1/3 c. smooth low-sodium peanut butter
- 1 teaspoon minced garlic
- 2 tbsps. Light soy sauce
- 1 tablespoon fresh lime juice
- 1 teaspoon brown sugar
- 1/3 c. water
- 2 tbsps. Chopped roasted

Air Fryer Baked Garlic Parsley Potatoes

BASIC RECIPE

NUTRITION

Calories 147
Carbs 26.7g
Fat 3.7g
Protein 3g.

4

15 MINUTES

35 MINUTES

SHOPPING LIST

- 3 russet potatoes
- 2 tbsps. Olive oil 1 tablespoon salt
- 1 tablespoon garlic powder
- 1 teaspoon parsley

DIRECTIONS

1. Rinse the potatoes under running water and pierce with a fork in several places.
2. Season with salt and garlic and drizzle with olive oil.
3. Rub the seasonings with your hands, so the potatoes are evenly coated.
4. Put the potatoes in the basket of your air fryer and slide them into the air fryer.
5. Set the temperature of 400°F and the timer for 35 minutes and turn the button On Check that they are cooked and once the potatoes are tender remove from the fryer.
6. Serve the potatoes garnished with chopped fresh parsley and topped with a dollop of sour cream.

Zucchini Parmesan Bites

BASIC RECIPES

SHOPPING LIST

- 4 medium zucchinis
- 1 c. grated coconuts
- 1 tablespoon italian seasoning
- ¼ chopped parsley
- ½ grated parmesan cheese
- 1 egg

10 MINUTES

10 MINUTES

1

NUTRITION

Calories 225	Protein 9g
Fat 17.9g	Carbs 10.6g

DIRECTIONS

1. Peel the zucchinis then cut into halves.
2. Discard the seeds then grate the zucchinis.
3. Place in a bowl.
4. Add grated coconuts, parsley, Italian seasoning, egg, and Parmesan cheese to the bowl. Mix well.
5. Shape the zucchini mixture into small balls forms then set aside.
6. Preheat an Air Fryer to 400°F (204°C).
7. Place a rack in the Air Fryer then arrange the zucchini balls on it.
8. Cook the zucchini balls for 10 minutes then remove them from heat.
9. Serve and enjoy.

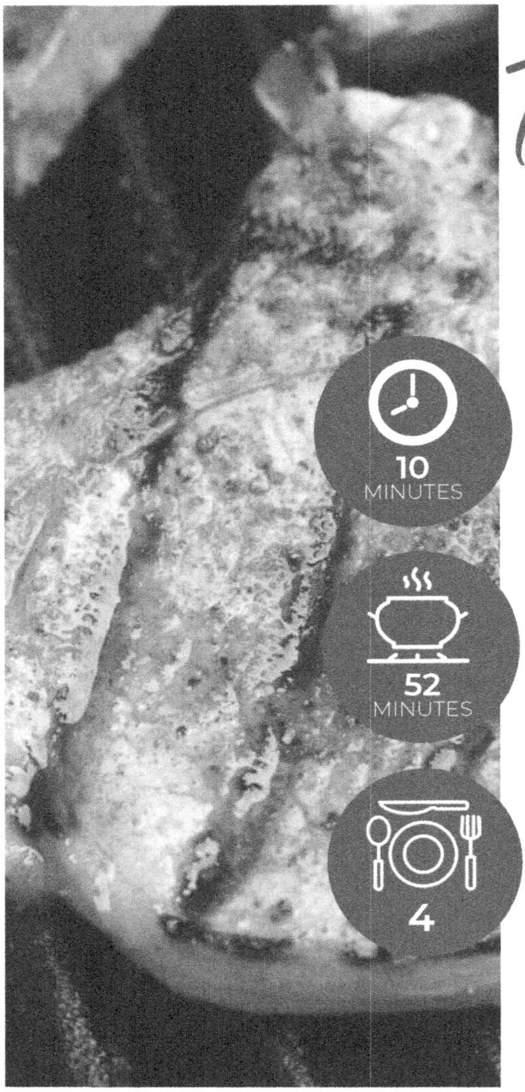

Bake Barbecued Pork Chops

INTERMEDIATE RECIPE

NUTRITION

Calories 489
Total Fat 17.75g
Total Carbs 41.74g
Fiber 0.8g
Protein 41.52g
Sugar 0.02g
Sodium 1482mg

SHOPPING LIST

- 4 bone-in pork chops, thick-cut
- Salt and black pepper to taste
- ½ tsp garlic powder
- ¼ tsp cayenne pepper
- ¼ cup brown sugar
- 2 tbsp honey - 1 cup ketchup
- ½ cup hot sauce
- 1 tsp apple cider vinegar
- ½ tsp paprika
- 1 tbsp Worcestershire sauce
- 1 tbsp yellow mustard
- ¼ tsp celery salt

DIRECTIONS

1. Preheat the oven at Bake mode at 350°F for 2 to 3 minutes and lightly grease an 8-inch baking dish (safe for the air fryer) with olive oil. Set aside.
2. Season the pork chops with salt, black pepper, and lay in the baking dish.
3. In a small bowl, mix the remaining ingredients and pour the mixture all over the meat while lifting the meat a little to have some of the spice mixes go under the chops.
4. Cover the dish with foil.
5. Slide the cooking tray upside down on the middle rack of the oven, place the baking dish on top and close the air fryer.
6. Set the timer for 45 or 50 minutes, and press Start. Cook until the timer reads to the end while opening the dish and turning the meat.
7. Once the timer ends, take off the foil, set the air fryer in Broil mode and press Start to brown the top of the pork.
8. When ready, remove the dish from the oven, allow sitting for 2 minutes and serve afterward.

SNACK

Simple Cauliflower Poppers

INTERMEDIATE RECIPE

NUTRITION

Calories 38
Total Fat 23.5 g
Saturated Fat 0.5 g
Cholesterol 0 mg
Sodium 49 mg
Total Carbs 1.8 g
Fiber 0.8 g
Sugar 0.8 g Protein 0.7 g

SHOPPING LIST

- ½ large head cauliflower, cut into bite-sized
- florets
- 1 tablespoon olive oil
- Salt and ground black pepper, as required

DIRECTIONS

1. In a bowl, add all the ingredients and toss to coat well.
2. Press "Power Button" of Air Fryer and turn the dial to select the "Air Fry" mode. Press
3. the Time button and again turn the dial to set the cooking time to 8 minutes.
4. Now push the Temp button and rotate the dial to set the temperature at 390°F.
5. Press "Start/Pause" button to start. When the unit beeps to
6. show that it is preheated, open the lid. Arrange the
7. cauliflower florets in "Air Fry Basket" and insert in the oven.
8. Toss the cauliflower florets once halfway through.
9. Serve warm.

Mixed Veggie Bites

BASIC RECIPE

SHOPPING LIST

- ¾ lb. fresh spinach, blanched, drained and
- chopped
- ¼ of onion, chopped
- ½ of carrot, peeled and chopped
- 1 garlic clove, minced
- 1 American cheese slice, cut into tiny pieces
- 1 bread slice, toasted and processed into
- breadcrumbs
- ½ tablespoon corn flour
- ½ teaspoon red chili flakes
- Salt, as required

NUTRITION

Calories 43
Total Fat 1.4 g
Saturated Fat 0.7 g
Cholesterol 3 mg
Sodium 155 mg
Total Carbs 5.6 g
Fiber 1.9 g
Sugar 1.2 g
Protein 3.1 g

15 MINUTES

10 MINUTES

DIRECTIONS

1. In a bowl, add all the ingredients except breadcrumbs and mix until well combined.
2. Add the breadcrumbs and gently stir to combine.
3. Make 10 equal-sized balls from the mixture.
4. Press "Power Button" of Air Fryer and turn the dial to select the "Air Fry" mode.
5. Press the Time button and again turn the dial to set the cooking time to 10 minutes.
6. Now push the Temp button and rotate the dial to set the temperature at 355⁰F.
7. Press the "Start/Pause" button to start.
8. When the unit beeps to show that it is preheated, open the lid.
9. Arrange the veggie balls in "Air Fry Basket"
10. and insert in the oven.
11. Serve warm.

5

Japanese Meatballs

INTERMEDIATE RECIPE

SHOPPING LIST

- 16 oz. ground beef
- 15 ml sesame oil
- 18g miso paste
- 10 fresh mint leaves, finely chopped
- 4 scallions, finely chopped
- 5g of salt
- 1 g black pepper
- 45 ml of soy sauce
- 45 ml mirin,
- 45 ml of water,
- 3g brown sugar

DIRECTIONS

1. Mix the ground beef, sesame oil, miso paste, mint leaves, chives, salt, and pepper until well combined.
2. Add a small amount of sesame oil to your hands and create 51 mm meatballs with the mixture.
3. You should have eight meatballs approximately. Let the meatballs cool in the refrigerator for 10 minutes.
4. Create the sauce by mixing the soy sauce, the mirin, the water, and the brown sugar. Leave aside.
5. Preheat the air fryer by pressing Start/Pause.
6. Arrange the chilled meatballs in the preheated air fryer.
7. Select Steak set the time to 10 minutes and press Start/ Pause.
8. Freely brush the meatballs with the glaze every 2 minutes.

10 MINUTES

25 MINUTES

3

NUTRITION

Calories 724
Fat 31g
Carbs 80g
Proteins: 31g
Sugar 0g

Mushroom Croquettes

INTERMEDIATE RECIPE

SHOPPING LIST

- 200g mushrooms
- ¼ of an onion
- Salt
- Nutmeg
- 3 large tbsps. of flour
- 4 tbsps. oil or
- 40g butter
- 1 liter of skim milk
- Breadcrumbs
- 2 eggs
- Flour

NUTRITION

Calories 54
Fat 2g
Carbs 7g
Protein 2
Sugar 1g
Cholesterol 12mg

5 MINUTES

25 MINUTES

4

DIRECTIONS

1. Chop the mushrooms and onion.
2. Brown the onion and mushrooms with a little oil in a pot, salt, and when golden brown, add two tablespoons of butter or a good stream of oil.
3. Add the tablespoons of flour and stir well until you get a very thick dough.
4. Gradually incorporate the milk (previously heated), until a dense mass is obtained.
5. Add salt and sprinkle with a pinch of nutmeg.
6. Let cool in the fridge for about two hours.
7. Make balls with the dough and pass through flour, egg, and breadcrumbs.
8. Preheat the air fryer a few minutes to 180^{0}C, and when ready, put the croquettes in the basket and set the timer for about 15 minutes at 180^{0}C.

Sausage Puff Pastry

INTERMEDIATE RECIPE

SHOPPING LIST

- Amount needed of puff pastry
- Amount needed of sausages

NUTRITION

Calories 135
Fat 11g
Carbs 5g
Protein 4g
Sugar 0g
Cholesterol 23mg

5 MINUTES

DIRECTIONS

1. Cut the puff pastry into thin slices about 5 cm wide.
2. Divide the sausages into two pieces.
3. Preheat the air fryer for a few minutes at 180°C. Meanwhile, roll each piece of sausage with a strip of puff pastry and paint it on top with a beaten egg.
4. Place in the basket of the air fryer.
5. Set the timer for 10 minutes at 180°C temperature.
6. Take as an appetizer at any time of the year. Kids love it.

20 MINUTES

1-4

Vanilla Soufflé

BASIC RECIPE

SHOPPING LIST

- ¼ cup butter, softened
- ¼ cup all-purpose flour
- ½ cup plus 2 tablespoons sugar, divided
- 1 cup milk
- 3 teaspoons vanilla extract, divided
- 4 egg yolks
- 5 egg whites
- 1 teaspoon cream of tartar
- 2 tablespoons powdered sugar plus extra for
- dusting

NUTRITION

Calories 250
Total Fat 11.6 g
Saturated Fat 6.5 g
Cholesterol 163 mg
Sodium 107 mg
Total Carbs 29.8 g
Fiber 0.1 g Sugar 25 g
Protein 6.8 g

DIRECTIONS

1. In a bowl, add the butter, and flour and mix until smooth paste forms.
2. In a medium pan, mix ½ cup of sugar and milk over medium-low heat and cook for about 3 minutes or until the sugar is dissolved, stirring continuously.
3. Add the flour mixture, whisking continuously, and simmer for about 3-4 minutes or until the mixture becomes thick.
4. Remove from the heat and stir in 1 teaspoon of vanilla extract.
5. Set aside for about 10 minutes to cool.
6. In a bowl, add the egg yolks and 1 teaspoon of vanilla extract and mix well.
7. Add the egg yolk mixture into the milk mixture and mix until well combined. In another bowl, add the egg whites, cream of tartar, remaining sugar, and vanilla extract and with a wire whisk, beat until stiff peaks form.
8. Fold the egg whites mixture into the milk mixture.
9. Grease 6 ramekins and sprinkle each with a pinch of sugar.
10. Place mixture into the prepared ramekins and with the back of a spoon, smooth the top surface.
11. Press "Power Button" of Air Fryer and turn the dial to select the "Air Fry" mode.
12. Press the Time button and again turn the dial to set the cooking time to 16 minutes.
13. Now push the Temp button and rotate the dial to set the temperature at 330^{0}F.
14. Press the "Start/Pause" button to start.
15. When the unit beeps to show that it is preheated, open the lid.
16. Arrange the ramekins in "Air Fry Basket" and insert them in the oven.
17. Place the ramekins onto a wire rack to cool slightly.
18. Sprinkle with the powdered sugar and serve warm.

15 MINUTES
23 MINUTES
6

Nutella Banana Muffins

INTERMEDIATE RECIPE

NUTRITION

Calories 227
Total Fat 6.6 g
Saturated Fat 1.5 g
Cholesterol 45 mg
Sodium 221 mg
Total Carbs 38.1 g
Fiber 2.4 g
Sugar 15.8 g
Protein 5.2 g

15 MINUTES

SHOPPING LIST

- 1 2/3 cups plain flour
- 1 teaspoon baking soda
- 1 teaspoon baking powder
- 1 teaspoon ground cinnamon
- ¼ teaspoon salt
- 4 ripe bananas, peeled and mashed, 2 eggs
- ½ cup brown sugar
- 1 teaspoon vanilla essence
- 3 tablespoons milk
- 1 tablespoon Nutella
- ¼ cup walnuts

DIRECTIONS

1. Grease 12 muffin molds. Set aside.
2. In a large bowl, sift together the flour, baking soda, baking powder, cinnamon, and salt.
3. In another bowl, mix the remaining ingredients except for walnuts.
4. Add the banana mixture into the flour mixture and mix until just combined.
5. Fold in the walnuts.
6. Place the mixture into the prepared muffin molds.
7. Press "Power Button" of Air Fryer and turn the dial to select the "Air Fry" mode.
8. Press the Time button and again turn the dial to set the cooking time to 25 minutes.
9. Now push the Temp button and rotate the dial to set the the temperature at 250°F.
10. Press the "Start/Pause" button to start.
11. When the unit beeps to show that it is preheated, open the lid.
12. Arrange the muffin molds in "Air Fry Basket" and insert in the oven.
13. Place the muffin molds onto a wire rack to cool for about 10 minutes.
14. Carefully, invert the muffins onto the wire rack to completely cool before serving.

25 MINUTES

12

Yummy Lemon bars

BASIC RECIPE

10 MINUTES

25 MINUTES

6

DIRECTIONS

1. In a bowl, mix butter with ½ cup Sugar and 2 cups flour, stir well, press on the bottom of a pan that fits your air fryer, introduce in the fryer and cook at 350⁰F for 10 minutes. In
2. another bowl, mix the rest of the Sugar with the rest of the flour, eggs and lemon juice, whisk, well and spread over crust.
3. Introduce in the fryer at 350⁰F for 15 minutes more, leave aside to cool down, cut bars and serve them.
4. Enjoy!

NUTRITION

Calories 125

Fat 4

Fiber 4

Carbs 16

Protein 2

SHOPPING LIST

- 4 eggs
- 2 and ¼ cups flour
- Juice from 2 lemons
- 1 cup butter, soft
- 2 cups Sugar

Pears and Espresso Cream

INTERMEDIATE RECIPE

10 MINUTES

30 MINUTES

4

DIRECTIONS

1. In a bowl, mix pears halves with lemon juice, 1 tablespoon Sugar, butter and water, toss well, transfer them to your air fryer and cook at 360°F for 30 minutes. Meanwhile, in a bowl, mix whipping cream with mascarpone, 1/3 cup Sugar and espresso, whisk well and keep in the fridge until pears are done.
2. Divide pears on plates, top with espresso cream and serve them.
3. Enjoy!

NUTRITION

Calories 211
Fat 5
Fiber 7
Carbs 8
Protein 7

SHOPPING LIST

- 4 pears, halved and cored
- 2 tablespoons lemon juice
- 1 tablespoon Sugar
- 2 tablespoons water
- 2 tablespoons butter
- For the cream:
- 1 cup whipping cream
- 1 cup mascarpone
- 1/3 cup Sugar
- 2 tablespoons espresso, cold

Poppy Seed Cake

INTERMEDIATE RECIPE

NUTRITION

Calories 211
Fat 6
Fiber 7
Carbs 12
Protein 6

SHOPPING LIST

- 1 and ¼ cups flour
- 1 teaspoon baking powder
- ¾ cup Sugar
- 1 tablespoon orange zest, grated
- 2 teaspoons lime zest, grated
- ½ cup butter, soft
- 2 eggs, whisked
- ½ teaspoon vanilla extract
- 2 tablespoons poppy seeds
- 1 cup milk
- For the Cream:
- 1 cup Sugar
- ½ cup passion fruit puree
- 3 tablespoons butter, melted
- 4 egg yolks

DIRECTIONS

1. In a bowl, mix flour with baking powder, ¾ cup Sugar, orange zest and lime zest and stir.
2. Add ½ cup butter, eggs, poppy seeds, vanilla and milk, stir using your mixer, pour into a cake pan that fits your air fryer and cook at 350°F for about 30 minutes.
3. Meanwhile, heat a pan with 3 tablespoons butter over medium heat, add Sugar and stir until it dissolves.
4. Take off heat, add passion fruit puree and egg yolks gradually and whisk well.
5. Take the cake out of the fryer, cool it down a bit and cut into halves horizontally.
6. Spread ¼ of passion fruit cream over one half, top with the other cake half and spread ¼ of the cream on top.
7. Serve cold.
8. Enjoy!

6

10 MINUTES

30 MINUTES

Ham Egg Cups

BASIC RECIPES

5 MINUTES

12 MINUTES

2

NUTRITION

Calories 382
Carb 4.6g
Fat 23.6g
Protein 29.4g

DIRECTIONS

1. Place 1 slice of ham on the bottom of 4 baking cups.
2. In a bowl, whisk eggs with sour cream.
3. Stir in onion, red pepper, and green pepper.
4. Pour the egg mixture into the baking cups.
5. Top with cheddar and place cups into the air fryer basket.Cook to 320^{0}F for 12 minutes.
6. Serve.

SHOPPING LIST

- 4 (1-ounce) slices of deli ham
- 4 eggs
- 2 tablespoons full-fat sour cream
- ¼ cup green bell pepper, diced
- 2 tablespoons red bell pepper, diced
- 2 tablespoons white onion, diced
- ½ cup shredded cheddar cheese

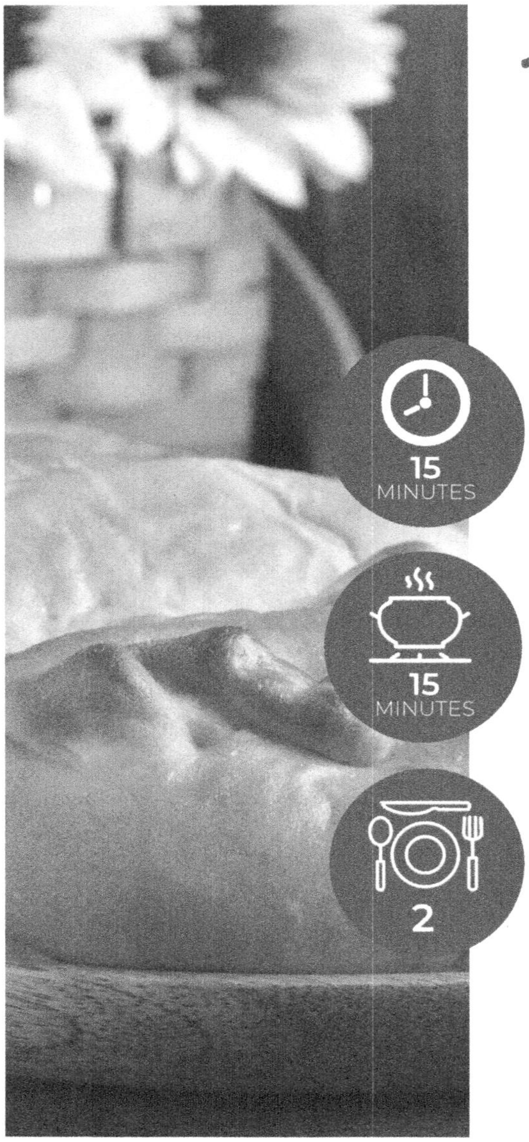

Breakfast Calzone

INTERMEDIATE RECIPE

NUTRITION

Calories 560
Carb: 4.2g
Fat 41.7g
Protein 34.5g

SHOPPING LIST

- ¾ cup shredded mozzarella cheese
- ¼ cup almond flour
- ½ ounce full-fat cream cheese
- 1 whole egg
- 2 eggs, scrambled
- ¼ pound breakfast sausage, cooked and crumbled
- 4 tablespoons shredded cheddar cheese

DIRECTIONS

1. Add almond flour, mozzarella, and cream cheese to a bowl. Microwave for 1 minute.
2. Stir until the mixture is smooth and forms a ball. Add the egg and stir until dough forms.
3. Place the dough between two sheets of parchment and roll out to a ¼-inch thickness. Cut the dough into four rectangles.
4. In a bowl, mix cooked sausage and scrambled eggs. Divide the blend between each piece of dough, placing it on the lower half of the rectangle.
5. Sprinkle each with cheddar. Fold to cover and seal the edges.
6. Cover the air fryer basket with parchment paper and cook at 380°F for 15 minutes.
7. Flip the calzones halfway through the cooking time.
8. Serve.

Grilled Sandwich with Three Types of Cheese

INTERMEDIATE RECIPE

NUTRITION

Calories 141 - Fat 1.01g
Carbs 68g - Protein 1.08g
Sugar 0.25g - Cholesterol 33mg

SHOPPING LIST

- 2 tablespoon mayonnaise
- ⅛ Teaspoon dried basil
- ⅛ Teaspoon dried oregano
- 4 slices of whole wheat bread
- 2 slices of ½ to 1-ounce cheddar cheese
- 2 slices of Monterey Jack cheese
- ½ to 1 ounce - 2 thin slices of tomato
- 2 slices of ½ to 1 oz. provolone cheese Soft butter

DIRECTIONS

1. Mix mayonnaise with basil and oregano in a small bowl and then spread the mixture on each side of the slice.
2. Cover each slice with a slice of each cheese and tomato, and then the other slice of bread.
3. Lightly brush each side of the sandwich and put the sandwiches in the basket.
4. Cook at a temperature of 400°F for 8 minutes, turning halfway through cooking

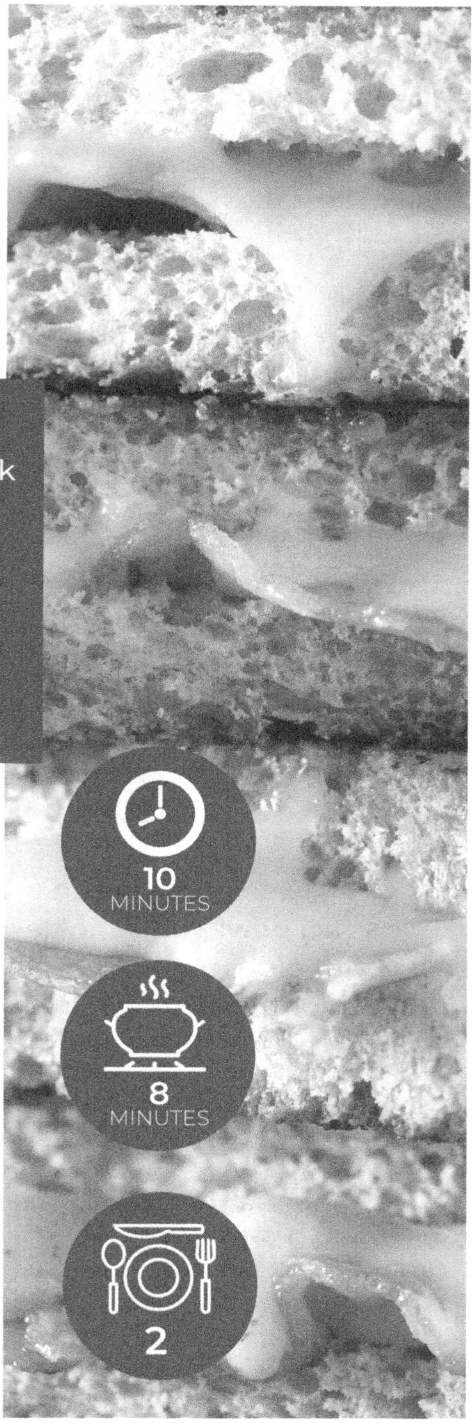

Sweet Nuts Butter

INTERMEDIATE RECIPE

SHOPPING LIST

- 1½ pounds sweet potatoes, peeled and cut
- into ½ inch pieces (2 medium)
- ½ tablespoon olive oil
- 1 tablespoon melted butter
- 1 tablespoon finely chopped walnuts
- ½ teaspoon grated one orange
- ⅛ Teaspoon nutmeg
- ⅛ Teaspoon ground cinnamon

NUTRITION

Calories 141
Fat 1.01g
Carbs 6.68g
Protein 1.08g
Sugar 0.25g
Cholesterol 7mg

5 MINUTES

25 MINUTES

5

DIRECTIONS

1. Put sweet potatoes in a small bowl and sprinkle with oil.
2. Stir until covered and then pour into the basket, ensuring that they are in a single layer.
3. Cook at a temperature of 350°F for 20 to 25 minutes, stirring or turning halfway through cooking.
4. Remove them to the serving plate.
5. Combine the butter, walnuts, orange zest, nutmeg, and cinnamon in a small bowl and pour the mixture over the sweet potatoes.

Zucchini & Walnut Cake with Maple Flavor Icing

EXPERT RECIPE

SHOPPING LIST

- 1 9-ounce package of yellow cake mix
- 1 egg
- ⅓ cup of water
- ½ cup grated zucchini
- ¼ cup chopped walnuts
- ¾ teaspoon of cinnamon
- ¼ teaspoon nutmeg
- ¼ teaspoon ground ginger maple flavor glaze

DIRECTIONS

1. Preheat the fryer to a temperature of 350°F.
2. Prepare an 8 x 3 7/8 inch loaf pan.
3. Prepare the cake dough according to package directions, using ⅓ cup of water instead of ½ cup.
4. Add zucchini, walnuts, cinnamon, nutmeg, and ginger.
5. Pour the dough into the prepared mold and put it inside the basket.
6. Bake until a toothpick inserted in the middle of the cake is clean when removed for 32 to 34 minutes.
7. Remove the cake from the fryer and let it cool on a grill for 10 minutes.
8. Then, remove the cake and place it on a serving plate.
9. Stop cooling just warm.
10. Spray it with maple flavor glaze.

5 MINUTES

35 MINUTES

5

NUTRITION

Calories 196
Carbs 27g
Fat 11g
Protein 1g
Sugar 7g
Cholesterol 0mg

Misto Quente

INTERMEDIATE RECIPE

SHOPPING LIST

- 4 slices of bread without shell
- 4 slices of turkey breast
- 4 slices of cheese
- 2 tablespoon cream cheese
- 2 spoons of butter

NUTRITION

Calories 340
Fat 15g
Carbs 32g
Protein 15g
Sugar 0g -
Cholesterol 0mg

5 MINUTES

10 MINUTES

4

DIRECTIONS

1. Preheat the air fryer. Set the timer of 5 minutes and the temperature to 200°C.
2. Pass the butter on one side of the slice of bread, and the other side of the slice, the cream cheese.
3. Mount the sandwiches are placing two slices of turkey breast and two slices of cheese between the pieces of bread, with the cream cheese inside and the side with butter.
4. Place the sandwiches in the basket of the air fryer.
5. Set the timer of the air fryer for 5 minutes and press the power button.

Bruschetta

BASIC RECIPE

NUTRITION

Calories 434
Fat 14g
Carbs 63g
Protein 11g
Sugar 8g
Cholesterol 0mg

DIRECTIONS

1. Preheat the air fryer.
2. Set the timer of 5 minutes and the temperature to 200°C.
3. Sprinkle the slices of Italian bread with olive oil.
4. Divide the chopped tomatoes and mozzarella between the slices. Season with salt, pepper, and oregano.
5. Put oil in the filling. Place a basil leaf on top of each slice.
6. Put the bruschetta in the basket of the air fryer being careful not to spill the filling.
7. Set the timer of 5 minutes, set the temperature to 180°C, and press the power button.
8. Transfer the bruschetta to a plate and serve.

SHOPPING LIST

- 4 slices of Italian bread
- 1 cup chopped tomato tea
- 1 cup grated mozzarella tea
- Olive oil
- Oregano, salt, and pepper
- 4 fresh basil leaves

5
MINUTES

10
MINUTES

2

Garlic Bread

BASIC RECIPE

SHOPPING LIST

- 2 stale French rolls
- 4 tablespoon crushed or crumpled garlic
- 1 cup of mayonnaise
- Powdered grated Parmesan
- 1 tablespoon olive oil

NUTRITION

Calories 340
Fat 15g
Carbs 32g
Protein 15g
Sugar 0g
Cholesterol 0mg

10 MINUTES

15 MINUTES

4-5

DIRECTIONS

1. Preheat the fryer. Set the time of 5 minutes and the temperature to 200ºC.
2. Mix mayonnaise with garlic and reserve.
3. Cut the baguettes into slices, but without separating them.
4. Fill the cavities of equals.
5. Brush with olive oil and sprinkle with grated cheese.
6. Place in the basket of the air fryer.
7. Set the timer to 10 minutes, set the temperature to 180ºC and press the power button.

Cream Buns with Strawberries

INTERMEDIATE RECIPE

NUTRITION

Calories 150
Fat 14g
Carbs 3g
Protein 11g
Sugar 8g
Cholesterol 0mg

10 MINUTES

SHOPPING LIST

- 240g all-purpose flour
- 50g granulated sugar
- 8g baking powder
- 1g of salt
- 85g chopped cold butter
- 84g chopped fresh strawberries
- 120 ml whipping cream
- 2 large eggs
- 10 ml vanilla extract
- 5 ml of water

DIRECTIONS

1. Sift flour, sugar, baking powder and salt in a large bowl.
2. Put the butter with the flour using a blender or your hands until the mixture resembles thick crumbs.
3. Mix the strawberries in the flour mixture.
4. Set aside for the mixture to stand.
5. Beat the whipping cream, 1 egg and the vanilla extract in a separate bowl.
6. Put the cream mixture in the flour mixture until they are homogeneous, then spread the mixture to a thickness of 38 mm.
7. Use a round cookie cutter to cut the buns.
8. Spread the buns with a combination of egg and water.
9. Set aside Preheat the air fryer, set it to 180°C.
10. Place baking paper in the preheated inner basket.
11. Place the buns on top of the baking paper and cook for 12 minutes at 180°C, until golden brown.

12 MINUTES

6

Blueberry Buns

INTERMEDIATE RECIPE

10 MINUTES

12 MINUTES

6

DIRECTIONS

1. Put sugar, flour, baking powder and salt in a large bowl.
2. Put the butter with the flour using a blender or your hands until the mixture resembles thick crumbs.
3. Mix the blueberries and ginger in the flour mixture and set aside.
4. Mix the whipping cream, 1 egg and the vanilla extract in a different container.
5. Put the cream mixture with the flour mixture until combined.
6. Shape the dough until it reaches a thickness of approximately 38 mm and cut it into eighths.
7. Spread the buns with a combination of egg and water. Set aside
8. Preheat the air fryer set it to 180°C.
9. Place baking paper in the preheated inner basket and place the buns on top of the paper.
10. Cook for 12 minutes at 180°C, until golden brown

SHOPPING LIST

- 240g all-purpose flour
- 50g granulated sugar
- 8g baking powder
- 2g of salt
- 85g chopped cold butter
- 85g of fresh blueberries
- 3g grated fresh ginger
- 113 ml whipping cream
- 2 large eggs
- 4 ml vanilla extract
- 5 ml of water

NUTRITION

Calories 105

Fat 1.64 g

Carbs 20.09 g

Protein 2.43 g

Sugar 2.1g

Cholesterol 0mg

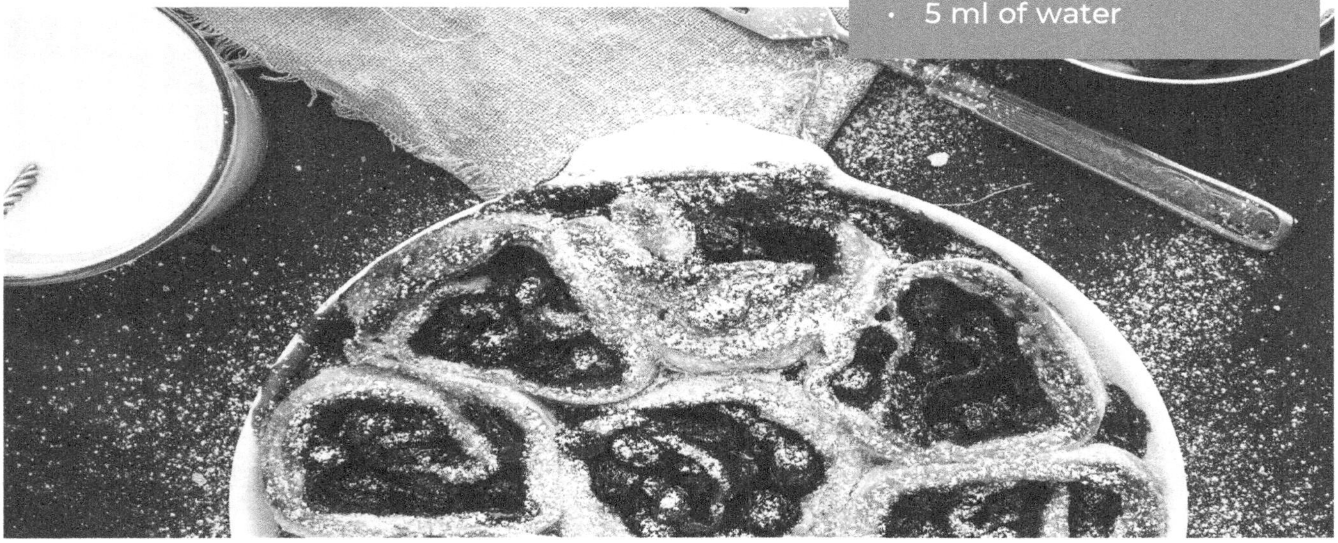

Cauliflower Potato Mash

BASIC RECIPE

15 MINUTES

15 MINUTES

4

DIRECTIONS

1. Add water to the saucepan and bring to boil.
2. Reduce heat and simmer for 10 minutes.
3. Drain vegetables well. Transfer vegetables,
4. butter, milk, and salt in a blender and blend until smooth.
5. Serve and enjoy.

SHOPPING LIST

- 2 cups potatoes, peeled and cubed
- 2 tablespoon butter
- ¼ cup milk
- 10 oz. cauliflower florets
- ¾ teaspoon salt

NUTRITION

Calories 128

Fat 6.2 g

Carbohydrates 16.3 g

Sugar 3.3 g

Protein 3.2 g

Cholesterol 17 mg

French Toast in Sticks

BASIC RECIPE

NUTRITION

Calories 128
Fat 6.2 g
Carbohydrates 16.3 g
Sugar 3.3 g
Protein 3.2 g
Cholesterol 17 mg

SHOPPING LIST

- 4 slices of white bread, 38 mm thick,
- preferably hard
- 2 eggs
- 60 ml of milk
- 15 ml maple sauce
- 2 ml vanilla extract
- Nonstick Spray Oil
- 38g of sugar
- 3ground cinnamon
- Maple syrup, to serve
- Sugar to sprinkle

DIRECTIONS

1. Cut each slice of bread into thirds making 12 pieces.
2. Lay on its side
3. Whisk in the eggs, milk, maple syrup and vanilla.
4. Preheat the air fryer, set it to 175°C.
5. Dip the sliced bread in the egg mixture and place it in the preheated deep fryer.
6. Sprinkle French toast generously with cooking spray.
7. Cook French toast for 10 minutes at 175°C.
8. Turn the toast halfway through cooking.
9. Mix the sugar and cinnamon in a bowl.
10. Coat the French toast with the sugar and cinnamon mixture when you are done cooking.
11. Serve with Maple syrup and sprinkle with powdered sugar

4

5 MINUTES

10 MINUTES

Breakfast Egg Tomato

BASIC RECIPES

NUTRITION

Calories 95
Sugar 5.1 g
Fat 5 g
Protein 7 g
Carbohydrates 7.5 g
Cholesterol 164 mg

10 MINUTES

24 MINUTES

2

DIRECTIONS

1. Preheat the air fryer to 325°F.
2. Cut off the top of a tomato and spoon out the tomato innards.
3. Break the egg in each tomato and place in the air fryer basket and cook for 24 minutes.
4. Season with parsley, pepper, and salt.
5. Serve and enjoy.

SHOPPING LIST

- 2 eggs
- 2 large fresh tomatoes
- 1 teaspoon fresh parsley
- Pepper
- Salt

10 MINUTES

32 MINUTES

4

Mushroom Leek Frittata

INTERMEDIATE RECIPE

NUTRITION

Calories 116
Fat 7 g
Carbohydrates 5.1 g
Sugar 2.1 g
Protein 10 g
Cholesterol 245 mg

SHOPPING LIST

- 6 eggs
- 6 oz. mushrooms, sliced
- 1 cup leeks, sliced
- Salt

DIRECTIONS

1. Preheat the air fryer to 325°F.
2. Spray air fryer baking dish with cooking spray and set aside.
3. Heat another skillet over medium heat.
4. Spray skillet with cooking spray.
5. Add mushrooms, leeks, and salt in a pan sauté for 6 minutes.
6. Break eggs in a bowl and whisk well.
7. Transfer sautéed mushroom and leek mixture into the prepared baking dish.
8. Pour egg over mushroom mixture.
9. Place dish in the air fryer and cook for 32 minutes.
10. Serve and enjoy.

Indian Cauliflower

INTERMEDIATE RECIPE

NUTRITION

Calories 49
Fat 0.5 g
Carbohydrates 9 g
Sugar 3 g
Protein 3 g
Cholesterol 0 mg

SHOPPING LIST

- 3 cups cauliflower florets
- 2 tbsps. water
- 2 teaspoon fresh lemon juice
- ½ tablespoon ginger paste
- 1 teaspoon chili powder
- ¼ teaspoon turmeric
- ½ cup vegetable stock
- Pepper
- Salt

DIRECTIONS

1. Add all ingredients into the air fryer baking dish and mix well.
2. Place dish in the air fryer and cook at 400°F for 10 minutes.
3. Stir well and cook at 360°F for 10 minutes more.
4. Stir well and serve.

Zucchini Salad

INTERMEDIATE RECIPE

SHOPPING LIST

- 1 lb. zucchini, cut into slices
- 2 tbsps. tomato paste
- ½ tablespoon tarragon, chopped
- 1 yellow squash, diced
- ½ lb. carrots, peeled and diced
- 1 tablespoon olive oil
- Pepper
- Salt

NUTRITION

Calories 79
Fat 3 g
Carbohydrates 11 g
Sugar 5 g
Protein 2 g
Cholesterol 0 mg

10 MINUTES

25 MINUTES

4

DIRECTIONS

1. In the air fryer baking dish mix together zucchini, tomato paste, tarragon, squash, carrots, pepper, and salt.
2. Drizzle with olive oil.
3. Place in the air fryer and cook at 400°F for 25 minutes.
4. Stir halfway through.
5. Serve and enjoy.

Bacon & Spinach Muffins

INTERMEDIATE RECIPE

SHOPPING LIST

- 6 eggs
- ½ cup milk
- Salt and ground black pepper, as required
- 1 cup fresh spinach, chopped
- 4 cooked bacon slices, crumbled

DIRECTIONS

1. In a bowl, add the eggs, milk, salt and black pepper and beat until well combined.
2. Add the spinach and stir to combine.
3. Divide the spinach mixture into 6 greased cups of an egg bite mold evenly.
4. Press "Power Button" of Air Fryer and turn the dial to select the "Air Fry" mode.
5. Press the Time button and again turn the dial to set the cooking time to 17 minutes.
6. Now push the Temp button and rotate the dial to set the temperature at 325°F.
7. Press the "Start/Pause" button to start.
8. When the unit beeps to show that it is preheated, open the lid.
9. Arrange the mold over the "Wire Rack" and insert it in the oven.
10. Place the mold onto a wire rack to cool for about 5 minutes.
11. Top with bacon pieces and serve warm.

10 MINUTES

17 MINUTES

6

NUTRITION

Calories 179 Total Fat 12.9 g
Saturated Fat 4.3g
Cholesterol 187 mg
Sodium 549 mg
Total Carbs 1.8 g
Fiber 0.1 g
Sugar 1.3 g
Protein 13.5 g

Ham Muffins

INTERMEDIATE RECIPE

SHOPPING LIST

- 6 ham slices
- 6 eggs
- 6 tablespoons cream
- 3 tablespoon mozzarella cheese, shredded
- ¼ teaspoon dried basil, crushed

NUTRITION

Calories 156
Total Fat 10 g
Saturated Fat 4.1 g
Cholesterol 189 mg
Sodium 516 mg
Total Carbs 2.3 g
Fiber 0.4g
Sugar 0.6 g
Protein 14.3 g

DIRECTIONS

1. Lightly, grease 6 cups of a silicone muffin tin.
2. Line each prepared muffin cup with 1 ham slice.
3. Crack 1 egg into each muffin cup and top with cream.
4. Sprinkle with cheese and basil.
5. Press "Power Button" of Air Fryer and turn the dial to select the "Air Fry" mode.
6. Press the Time button and again turn the dial to set the cooking time to 18 minutes.
7. Now push the Temp button and rotate the dial to set the the temperature at 350°F.
8. Press the "Start/Pause" button to start.
9. When the unit beeps to show that it is preheated, open the lid.
10. Arrange the muffin tin over the "Wire Rack" and insert it in the oven.
11. Place the muffin tin onto a wire rack to cool for about 5 minutes.
12. Carefully, invert the muffins onto the platter and serve warm.

10 MINUTES

18 MINUTES

6

Savory Carrot Muffins

BASIC RECIPE

NUTRITION

Calories 292
Total Fat 13.1 g
Saturated Fat 5.7 g
Cholesterol 25 mg
Sodium 579 mg
Total Carbs 27.2 g
Fiber 1.5 g
Sugar 2 g
Protein 17.7 g

15 MINUTES

SHOPPING LIST

- For Muffins:
- ¼ cup whole-wheat flour
- ¼ cup all-purpose flour
- ½ teaspoon baking powder
- 1/8 teaspoon baking soda
- ½ teaspoon dried parsley, crushed
- ½ teaspoon salt
- ½ cup plain yogurt
- 1 teaspoon vinegar
- 1 tablespoon vegetable oil
- 3 tablespoons cottage cheese, grated
- 1 carrot, peeled and grated
- 2-4 tablespoons water (if needed)
- For Topping:
- 7 oz. Parmesan cheese, grated
- ¼ cup walnuts, chopped

DIRECTIONS

1. For muffin: in a large bowl, mix the flours, baking powder, baking soda, parsley, and salt.
2. In another large bowl, mix well the yogurt, and vinegar.
3. Add the remaining ingredients except for water and beat them well. (add some water if needed)
4. Make a well in the center of the yogurt mixture.
5. Slowly, add the flour mixture in the well and mix until well combined.
6. Place the mixture into lightly greased muffin molds evenly and top with the Parmesan cheese and walnuts.
7. Press "Power Button" of Air Fryer and turn the dial to select the "Air Fry" mode.
8. Press the Time button and again turn the dial to set the cooking time to 7 minutes.
9. Now push the Temp button and rotate the dial to set the temperature at 355°F. Press "Start/Pause" button to start.
10. When the unit beeps to show that it is preheated, open the lid.
11. Arrange the ramekins over "Wire Rack" and insert them in the oven.
12. Place the muffin molds onto a wire rack to cool for about 5 minutes.
13. Carefully, invert the muffins onto the platter and serve warm with your desired toppings.

7 MINUTES

6

Salsa Eggs

BASIC RECIPE

NUTRITION

Calories 142
Carb: 5.4g
Fat 9.4g
Protein 9.8g

SHOPPING LIST

- ½ green bell pepper, chopped
- ½ red bell pepper, chopped
- 2 eggs, whisked
- 1 tablespoon mild salsa
- Cooking spray
- ½ tablespoon chives, chopped
- Salt and black pepper, to taste
- ¼ cup cheddar cheese, grated

DIRECTIONS

1. Grease 2 ramekins with cooking spray and divide the bell peppers into each.
2. In a bowl, mix the eggs with the salsa, chives, salt, and pepper and whisk well.
3. Divide the egg mixture between each ramekin and sprinkle the cheese on top.
4. Preheat the air fryer at 360°F. Arrange the ramekins in the frying basket.
5. Cook for 20 minutes at 360°F.
6. Serve.

5 MINUTES

20 MINUTES

2

Banana Oats

BASIC RECIPE

NUTRITION

Calories 533
Fat 25.8g
Carb: 57.9g
Protein 11.5g

5 MINUTES

SHOPPING LIST

- 1 cup old fashioned oats
- ½ teaspoon baking powder
- 2 tablespoons sugar
- ½ teaspoon vanilla extract
- 1 banana, peeled and mashed
- ½ cup milk
- ½ cup heavy cream
- 1 egg, whisked
- 1 tablespoon butter
- Cooking spray

DIRECTIONS

1. In a bowl, mix the oats with the baking powder, sugar, and other ingredients except for the cooking spray and whisk well.
2. Divide the mixture into 2 ramekins.
3. Grease the air fryer with cooking spray and preheat at 340^{0}F.
4. Place the ramekins in the air fryer and cook for 20 minutes.
5. Serve.

20 MINUTES

2

Jalapeno Popper Egg Cups

INTERMEDIATE RECIPE

DIRECTIONS

1. Beat the eggs in a bowl, then pour into four silicon muffin cups.
2. In a bowl, add cream cheese, jalapenos, and
3. cheddar. Microwave for 30 seconds and stir.
4. Take about ¼ of the mixture and place it in
5. the center of one egg cup.
6. Repeat with the remaining mixture.
7. Place egg cups into the air fryer basket.
8. Cook at 320^{0}F for 10 minutes.
9. Serve.

10 MINUTES

10 MINUTES

2

SHOPPING LIST

- 4 eggs
- ¼ cup pickled jalapenos, chopped
- 2 ounces full-fat cream cheese
- ½ cup shredded sharp cheddar cheese

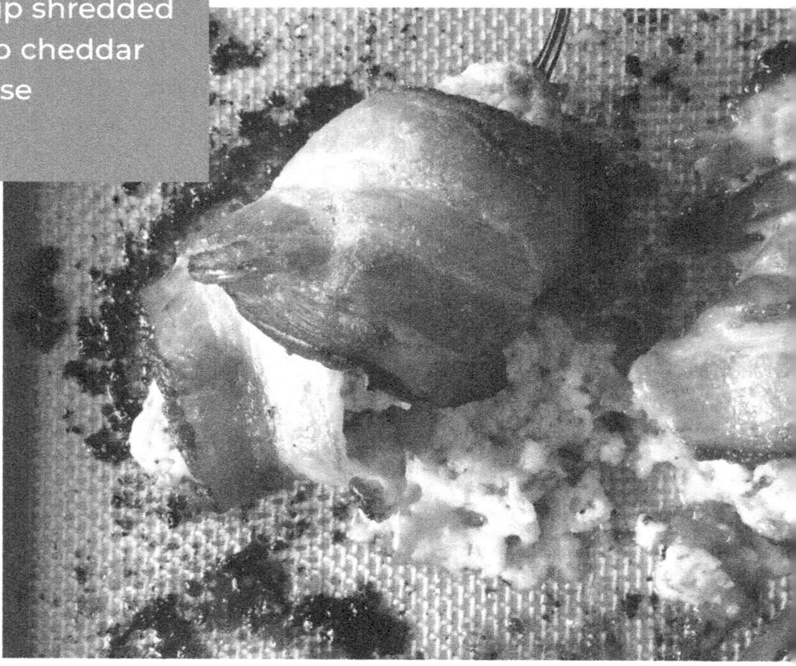

NUTRITION

Calories 354
Carb: 2g
Fat 25.3g
Protein 21g

Cheese Sandwich

BASIC RECIPE

DIRECTIONS

1. Place 2 cheese slices between the 2 bread slices and spread the butter on the outside of both pieces of bread. Repeat to assemble the remaining sandwich.
2. Place sandwiches in the air fryer basket and cook at 370°F for 8 minutes.
3. Turn halfway through.
4. Serve.

5 MINUTES

8 MINUTES

2

SHOPPING LIST

- 4 cheddar cheese slices
- 4 teaspoons butter
- 4 bread slices

NUTRITION

Calories 341
Carb: 9.8g
Fat 26.8g
Protein 5g

French Toast

BASIC RECIPE

NUTRITION

Calories 166
Carb: 16.5g
Fat 6.7g
Protein 9.7g

SHOPPING LIST

- 4 bread slices
- 1 tablespoon powdered cinnamon
- 1 teaspoon vanilla extract
- ⅔ Cup milk
- 2 eggs

DIRECTIONS

1. In a bowl, combine eggs, vanilla, cinnamon, and milk. Mix well.
2. Dip each bread slice into the egg mixture and shake off excess.
3. Place bread slices in a pan.
4. Place pan in the air fryer and cook at 320⁰F for 3 minutes.
5. Flip and cook for 3 more minutes, then serve.

2

5 MINUTES

6 MINUTES

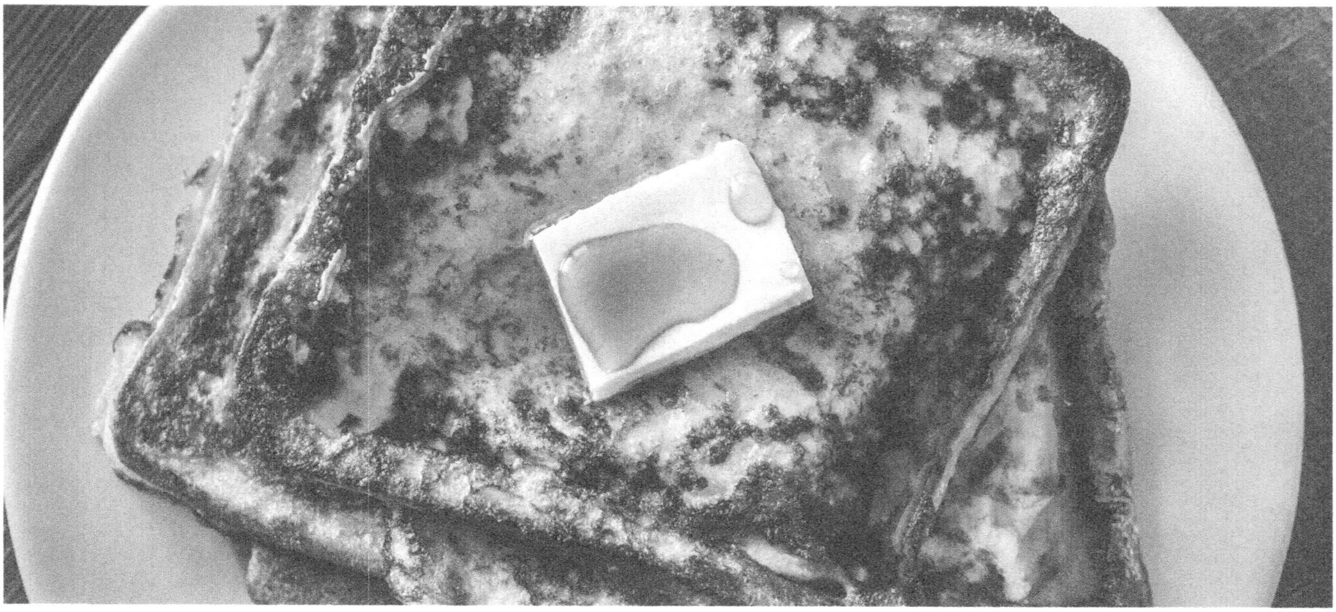

Breakfast Sausage Frittata

BASIC RECIPES

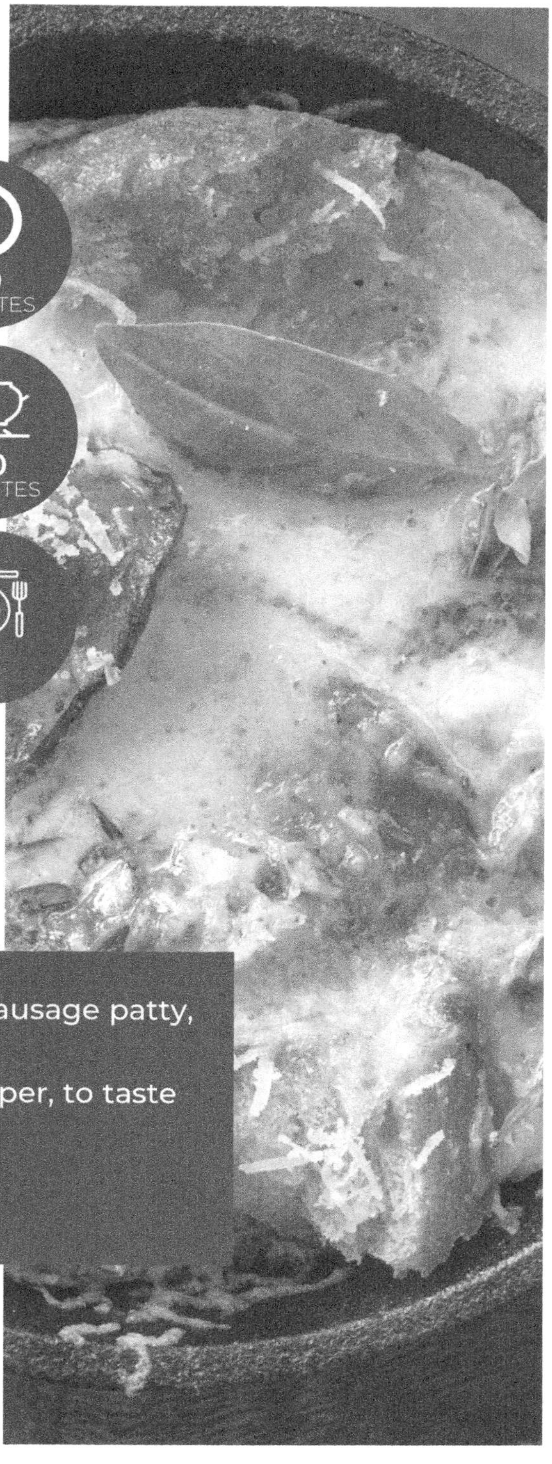

NUTRITION

Calories 206
Fat 14.7g
Carb: 6.7g
Protein 12.8g

DIRECTIONS

1. Spray a 4-inch mini pan with cooking spray and set aside.
2. Add chopped sausage patty to a Preparation Timeared dish and air fry at 350⁰F for 5 minutes.
3. Meanwhile, in a bowl, whisk the eggs, pepper, and salt.
4. Add bell peppers, spring onions, and mix well.
5. Once the sausage is done, add them to the egg mixture and mix well, then pour the mixture into the 4-inch pan.
6. Sprinkle with cheese and air fry at 350⁰F for 5 minutes. Serve.

SHOPPING LIST

- Cooking Spray
- 2 eggs
- 2 tablespoons cheddar cheese
- 1 bell pepper, chopped
- 1 tablespoon spring onions, chopped
- 1 breakfast sausage patty, chopped
- Salt and pepper, to taste

Scrambled Eggs & Toasted Bread

BASIC RECIPE

5 MINUTES

9 MINUTES

2

NUTRITION

Calories 150
Carb: 5.2g
Fat 9.1g
Protein 11.8g

SHOPPING LIST

- 4 eggs
- 2 bread slices
- Salt and pepper, to taste

DIRECTIONS

1. Warm bread slices in the air fryer at 400°F for 3 minutes.
2. Add eggs to a pan and season with salt and pepper. Mix well.
3. Place pan in the air fryer and cook at 360°F for 2 minutes.
4. Stir quickly and cook for 4 more minutes.
5. Stir well and transfer the scrambled eggs over the toasted bread slices.
6. Serve.

Egg, Spinach, and Sausage Cups

INTERMEDIATE RECIPE

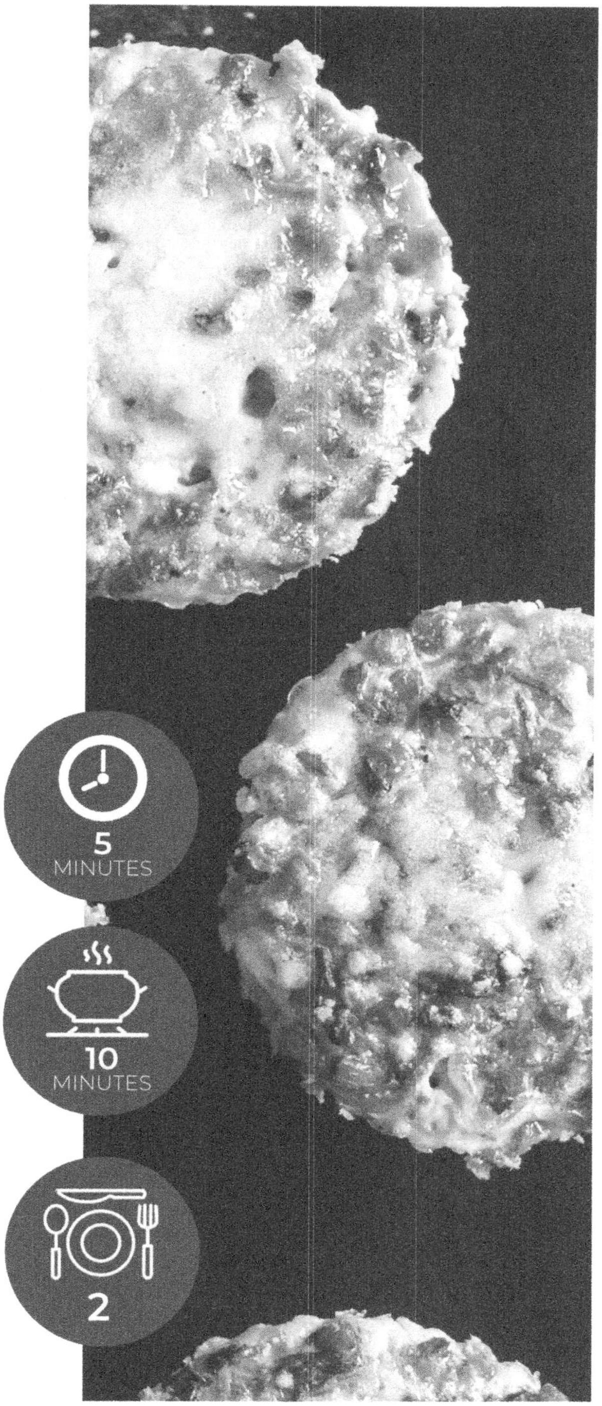

NUTRITION

Calories 89

Fat 6.3g

Carb: 1g

Protein 7g

SHOPPING LIST

- ¼ cup eggs, beaten
- 4 teaspoons shredded jack cheese
- 4 tablespoons spinach, chopped
- 4 tablespoons sausage, cooked and crumbled
- Salt and pepper

DIRECTIONS

1. Whisk everything together in a bowl and mix well.
2. Pour batter into muffin cups and place them in the air fryer basket.
3. Bake at 330°F for 10 minutes.
4. Cool and serve.

Turkey Burrito

INTERMEDIATE RECIPE

SHOPPING LIST

- 4 slices turkey breast, cooked
- ½ red bell pepper, sliced
- 2 eggs
- 1 small avocado, peeled, pitted, and sliced
- 2 tablespoons salsa
- Salt and black pepper, to taste
- ⅛ Cup mozzarella cheese, grated
- Tortillas for serving

NUTRITION

Calories 349
Fat 23g
Carb: 20g
Protein 21g

10 MINUTES

10 MINUTES

2

DIRECTIONS

1. In a bowl, whisk the eggs with salt and pepper.
2. Pour them into a pan and place them in the air fryer's basket.
3. Cook at 400°F for 5 minutes.
4. Remove from the fryer and transfer eggs to a plate.
5. Arrange tortillas on a working surface.
6. Divide eggs, turkey meat, bell pepper, cheese, salsa, and avocado between them.
7. Roll the burritos.
8. Line the air fryer basket with tin foil and place the burritos inside.
9. Heat the burritos at 300°F for 3 minutes.
10. Serve.

Breakfast Bread Pudding

INTERMEDIATE RECIPE

SHOPPING LIST

- ¼ pound white bread, cubed
- 6 tablespoons milk
- 6 tablespoons water
- 1 teaspoon cornstarch
- ¼ cup apple, peeled, cored, and chopped
- 2 ½ tablespoons honey
- ½ teaspoon vanilla extract
- 1 teaspoon cinnamon powder
- ¾ cup flour
- ⅓ Cup brown sugar
- 1 ½ ounces soft butter

DIRECTIONS

1. In a bowl, combine bread, apple, cornstarch, vanilla, cinnamon, honey, milk, and water.
2. Whisk well.
3. In another bowl, combine butter, sugar, and flour and mix well.
4. Press half of the crumble mixture into the bottom of the air fryer, add bread and apple mixture, and then add the rest of the crumble.
5. Cook at 350°F for 22
6. minutes. Divide bread pudding onto plates and serve.

NUTRITION

Calories 261
Fat 7g
Carb: 8g
Protein 5g

10 MINUTES

22 MINUTES

2

Eggs in Avocado Boats

INTERMEDIATE RECIPE

SHOPPING LIST

- 1 large avocado, cut in half lengthwise
- 2 eggs
- Salt and pepper, to taste
- 1 cup cheddar, shredded
- 1 teaspoon parsley

NUTRITION

Calories 450
Fat 35g
Carb: 6g
Protein 25g

5 MINUTES

6 MINUTES

2

DIRECTIONS

1. Preheat the air fryer at 300°F.
2. In a bowl, crack the eggs and mix with the pulp of avocado after de-seeding it.
3. Add salt, pepper, and shredded cheddar.
4. Pour the mixture into the empty avocado halves.
5. Cook in the air fryer for 5 minutes.
6. Sprinkle with chopped parsley and serve.

Toast Less Sausage in Egg Pond

BASIC RECIPE

NUTRITION

Calories 26
Carbs 4.2g
Protein 18.3g
Fat 18.8g

20 MINUTES

DIRECTIONS

1. Whip the eggs with cream in a bowl.
2. Pour the egg mixture into the ramekins and fold in the sausage and bread slices.
3. Top both cheese.
4. Place the ramekins in the cooking tray.
5. Set the Air fryer to 365°F for 20 minutes.
5. Insert the cooking tray in the Air Fryer when it displays "Add Food".
6. Remove from the oven when cooking time is complete.
7. Serve warm.

SHOPPING LIST

- 1 bread slice, cut into sticks
- 3 eggs
- 2 cooked sausages, sliced
- 1/8 cup of Parmesan cheese, grated
- ¼ cup of cream
- 1/8 cup of mozzarella cheese, grated

20 MINUTES

4

Flavorful Bacon Cup

INTERMEDIATE RECIPE

NUTRITION

Calories 260
Protein 16.1g
Carbs 6.9g
Fat 18g

10 MINUTES

SHOPPING LIST

- 6 bacon slices
- 6 bread slices
- 1 scallion, chopped
- 2 cups of pecans, finely chopped
- 3 tablespoons of green bell pepper, seeded
- and chopped
- 6 eggs
- 2 tablespoons of low-fat mayonnaise

DIRECTIONS

1. Place the bacon slices at the bottom of 6 greased muffin tins.
2. Cut the bread slices into round shapes and place them over the bacon slices.
3. Top with scallion, bell pepper, and mayonnaise.
4. Crack eggs over the top and arrange the muffin tins in the cooking tray.
5. Set the Air fryer to 375^{0}F for 15 minutes.
6. Insert the cooking tray in the Air Fryer when it displays "Add Food".
7. Remove from the oven when cooking time is complete. Serve warm.

15 MINUTES

6

Banana Bread

INTERMEDIATE RECIPE

NUTRITION

Calories 295
Carbs 44g
Protein 3.1g
Fat 13.3g

DIRECTIONS

1. Cream together all the wet ingredients in a bowl.
2. Strain together all the dry ingredients in another bowl.
3. Mix well to form a dough and place in the loaf pan.
4. Place the loaf pan in the cooking tray.
5. Set the the Air fryer to 335°F for 20 minutes.
6. Insert the cooking tray in the Air Fryer when it displays "Add Food".
7. Remove from the oven when cooking time is complete.
8. Serve warm.

SHOPPING LIST

- 3 bananas, peeled and sliced
- 2/3 cup sugar
- 1 teaspoon of ground cinnamon
- 1 teaspoon of salt
- 1 1/3 cups of flour
- 1 teaspoon of baking soda
- 1 teaspoon of baking powder
- ½ cup of milk
- ½ cup of olive oil

10 MINUTES

20 MINUTES

8

Crispy Potato Rosti

INTERMEDIATE RECIPE

10 MINUTES

15 MINUTES

2

DIRECTIONS

1. Mingle the potatoes, shallots, cheese, chives, salt, and black pepper in a large bowl.
2. Place this potato mixture in the cooking tray and drizzle with olive oil.
3. Set the Air fryer to 365⁰F for 15 minutes.
4. Insert the cooking tray in the Air Fryer when it displays "Add Food".
5. Remove from the oven when cooking time is complete.
6. Slice the potato rosti into wedges and top with sour cream and salmon slices to serve.

SHOPPING LIST

- 1/8 cup of cheddar cheese
- 3.5 ounces of smoked salmon, cut into slices
- 2 tablespoons of sour cream
- ½ pound of russet potatoes, peeled and
- grated roughly
- 1 tablespoon of chives, chopped finely
- 2 tablespoons of shallots, minced
- 1 tablespoon of olive oil
- Salt and black pepper, to taste

NUTRITION

Calories 327
Carbs 23.3
Protein 15.3
Fat 20.2

Stylish Ham Omelet

BASIC RECIPE

DIRECTIONS

1. Put onion and ham on medium heat in a nonstick skillet. Sauté for about 5 minutes and place in the cooking tray along with the tomatoes.
2. Whip eggs with salt and black pepper in a bowl.
3. Drizzle the egg mixture in the cooking tray and top with the cheddar cheese.
4. Set the Air fryer to 390^{0}F for 10 minutes. Insert the cooking tray in the Air Fryer when it displays “Add Food"
5. Remove from the oven when cooking time is complete.
6. Serve warm with toasts.

10 MINUTES

30 MINUTES

2

NUTRITION

Calories 255	Carbs 14.1g
Protein 19.7g	Fat 13.9g

SHOPPING LIST

- 1 onion, chopped
- 2 tablespoons of cheddar cheese
- 4 small tomatoes, chopped
- 2 ham slices
- Salt and black pepper, to taste
- 4 eggs

Healthy Tofu Omelet

BASIC RECIPE

NUTRITION

Calories 248
Carbs 6.5g
Protein 20.4g
Fat 15.9g

DIRECTIONS

1. Put the olive oil, onion, and garlic in a skillet and sauté for about 3 minutes.
2. Stir in the chives, tofu, and mushrooms.
3. Sprinkle with salt and black pepper.
4. Whisk the eggs and drizzle over the chives mixture.
5. Pour this mixture into the cooking tray.
6. Set the Air fryer to 360^{0}F for 22 minutes.
7. Insert the cooking tray in the Air Fryer when it displays "Add Food".
8. Poke the eggs twice in between and remove them from the oven when cooking time is complete. Serve warm.

SHOPPING LIST

- 1 tablespoon of chives, chopped
- 1 garlic clove, minced
- 2 teaspoons of olive oil
- 1 cup mushroom
- ¼ of onion, chopped
- 12-ounce of silken tofu, pressed and sliced
- 3 eggs, beaten
- Salt and black pepper, to taste

4

5 MINUTES

22 MINUTES

Peanut Butter Banana Bread

BASIC RECIPES

NUTRITION

Calories 384   Carbs 39.3g
Protein 8.9g   Fat 2.6g

15 MINUTES

30 MINUTES

6

SHOPPING LIST

- 2 medium ripe bananas, peeled and mashed
- ¾ cup of walnuts, roughly chopped
- ¼ teaspoon of salt
- 1/3 cup of granulated sugar
- 1 cup plus 1 tablespoon of all-purpose flour
- 1¼ teaspoons of baking powder
- ¼ cup of canola oil
- 2 tablespoons of creamy peanut butter
- 2 tablespoons of sour cream
- 1 teaspoon of vanilla extract
- 1 large egg
- 6 cups of tea (for serving)

DIRECTIONS

1. Set the Air fryer to 330^{0}F for 40 minutes. Strain together with the baking powder, flour, and salt in a bowl.
2. Cream together eggs with sugar, canola oil, sour cream, peanut butter, and vanilla extract in another bowl.
3. Fold in the flour mixture, bananas, and walnuts until thoroughly combined.
4. Pour the mixture into the baking dish and place in the cooking tray.
5. Insert the cooking tray in the Air Fryer when it displays "Add Food".
6. Remove from the oven when cooking time is complete. Slice the bread as desired and serve with tea.

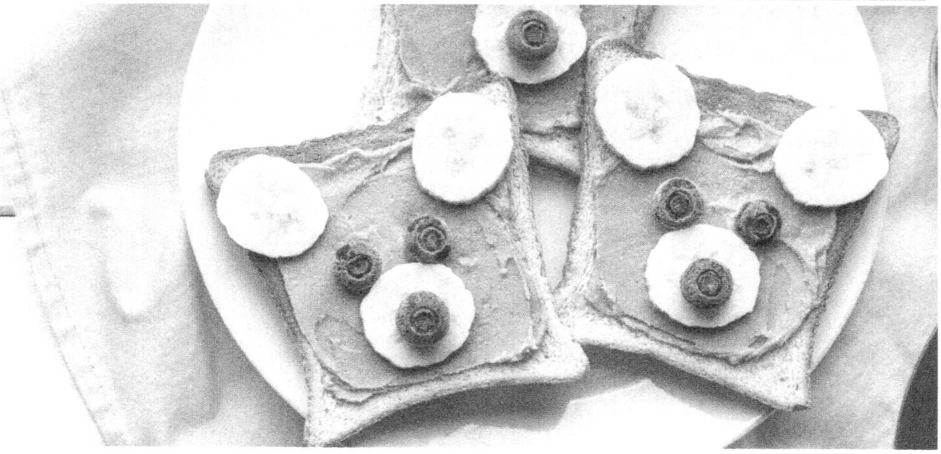

Aromatic Potato Hash

BASIC RECIPE

NUTRITION

Calories 229
Carbs 30.8g
Protein 10.3g
Fat 7.6g

SHOPPING LIST

- 1 medium onion, chopped
- ½ teaspoon of thyme leaves, crushed
- 5 eggs, beaten
- 2 teaspoons of butter, melted
- Salt and black pepper, to taste
- ½ of green bell pepper, seeded and chopped
- 1½ pound of russet potatoes, peeled and
- cubed
- ½ teaspoon of dried savory, crushed

DIRECTIONS

1. Set the Air fryer to 390^{0}F for 30 minutes.
2. Put the onion, bell pepper, thyme, potatoes, savory, salt, and black pepper in a cooking tray. Insert the cooking tray in the Air fryer when it displays "Add Food".
3. Remove from the oven when cooking time is complete. Meanwhile, add butter and whisked eggs in a skillet.
4. Sauté for about 1 minute on each side and place the egg pieces into the cooking tray.
5. Cook in the Air fryer again for about 5 minutes and dish out to serve.

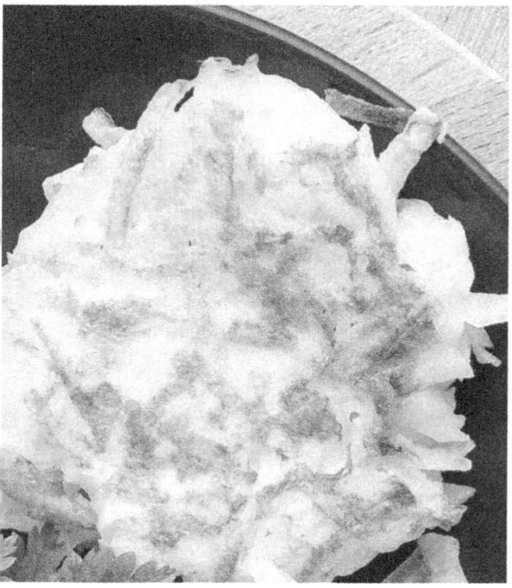

Pumpkin & Yogurt Bread

INTERMEDIATE RECIPE

NUTRITION

Calories 212
Carbs 36g
Protein 6.6g
Fat 3.4g

SHOPPING LIST

- 2 large eggs
- 6 tablespoons of oats
- 4 tablespoons of honey
- 2 tablespoons of vanilla essence
- 8 tablespoons of pumpkin puree
- 6 tablespoons of banana flour
- 4 tablespoons of plain Greek yogurt
- Pinch of ground nutmeg

DIRECTIONS

1. Set the Air fryer to 360°F for 15 minutes. Blend all the ingredients in a bowl except oats with an electric mixer.
2. Stir in the oats and transfer them into the cooking tray. Insert the cooking tray in the Air fryer when it displays “Add Food”.
3. Remove from oven when cooking time is complete.
4. Slice into desired pieces to serve.

10 MINUTES

15 MINUTES

4

Zucchini Fritters

BASIC RECIPE

SHOPPING LIST

- ¼ cup of all-purpose flour
- 2 eggs
- 1 teaspoon of fresh dill, minced
- 7 ounces of Halloumi cheese
- Salt and black pepper, to taste
- 10½ ounces of zucchini, grated and squeezed

NUTRITION

Calories 250
Protein 15.2g
Carbs 10g
Fat 17.2g

4
MINUTES

7
MINUTES

1

DIRECTIONS

1. Set the Air fryer to 360^{0}F for 7 minutes.
2. Combine all the ingredients in a bowl.
3. Form fritter from this mixture and place on the cooking tray.
4. Insert the cooking tray in the Air fryer when it displays “Add Food”.
5. Remove from the oven when cooking time is complete.
6. Serve warm.

Muffins Sandwich

INTERMEDIATE RECIPE

SHOPPING LIST

- Nonstick Spray Oil
- 1 slice of white cheddar cheese
- 1 slice of Canadian bacon
- 1 English muffin, divided
- 15 ml hot water
- 1 large egg
- Salt and pepper to taste

DIRECTIONS

1. Spray the inside of an 85g mold with oil spray and place it in the air fryer.
2. Preheat the air fryer, set it to 160°C.
3. Add the Canadian cheese and bacon and white cheddar cheese to the preheated air fryer.
4. Pour the hot water and the egg into the hot pan and season with salt and pepper.
5. Select Bread, set to 10 minutes.
6. Take out the English muffins after 7 minutes, leaving the egg for the full time.
7. Build your sandwich by placing the cooked egg on top of the English muffing and serve.

2 MINUTES

10 MINUTES

1

NUTRITION

400 Fat 26g
Carbohydrates 26g
Sugar 15 g
Protein 3 g
Cholesterol 155 mg

Bacon BBQ

BASIC RECIPE

SHOPPING LIST

- 13g dark brown sugar
- 5g chili powder
- 1g ground cumin
- 1g cayenne pepper
- 4 slices of bacon, cut in half

NUTRITION

Calories 1124
Fat 72g
Carbs 59g
Protein 49g
Sugar 11g
Cholesterol 77mg

2 MINUTES

8 MINUTES

2

DIRECTIONS

1. Mix seasonings until well combined.
2. Dip the bacon in the dressing until it is completely covered. Leave aside.
3. Preheat the air fryer, set it to 160°C.
4. Place the bacon in the preheated air fryer
5. Select Bacon and press Start/Pause.

Stuffed French toast

INTERMEDIATE RECIPE

NUTRITION

Calories 159
Fat 7.5g
Carbs 25.2g
Protein 14g
Sugar 0g
Cholesterol 0mg

DIRECTIONS

1. Preheat the air fryer, set it to 175°C.
2. Make a cut in the middle of the muffin.
3. Fill the inside of the slit with cream cheese. Leave aside.
4. Mix the eggs, milk, whipping cream, sugar, cinnamon, and vanilla extract.
5. Moisten the stuffed French toast in the egg mixture for 10 seconds on each side.
6. Sprinkle each side of French toast with oil spray.
7. Place the French toast in the preheated air fryer and cook for 10 minutes at 175°C
8. Stir the French toast carefully with a spatula when you finish cooking.
9. Serve topped with chopped pistachios and maple syrup.

SHOPPING LIST

- 1 slice of brioche bread,
- 64 mm thick, preferably rancid
- 113g cream cheese
- 2 eggs
- 15 ml of milk
- 30 ml whipping cream
- 38g of sugar
- 3g cinnamon
- 2 ml vanilla extract
- nonstick spray oil
- pistachios chopped to cover
- maple syrup, to serve

4 MINUTES

10 MINUTES

1

Breakfast Pizza

INTERMEDIATE RECIPE

NUTRITION

Calories 224
Fat 7.5g
Carbs 25.2g
Protein 14g
Sugar 0g
Cholesterol 13mg

5 MINUTES

SHOPPING LIST

- 10 ml of olive oil
- 1 prefabricated pizza dough (178 mm)
- 28g low moisture mozzarella cheese
- 2 slices smoked ham
- 1 egg
- 2g chopped cilantro

DIRECTIONS

1. Pass olive oil over the prefabricated pizza dough.
2. Add mozzarella cheese and smoked ham to the dough.
3. Preheat the air fryer, set it to 175°C.
4. Place the pizza in the preheated air fryer and cook for 8 minutes at 175°C.
5. Remove the baskets after 5 minutes and open the egg on the pizza.
6. Replace the baskets in the air fryer and finish cooking.
7. Garnish with chopped cilantro and serve.

8 MINUTES

1-2

Nutty Zucchini Bread

BASIC RECIPE

15 MINUTES

NUTRITION

Calories 377
Carbs 47.9g
Protein 5.5g
Fat 19.3g

SHOPPING LIST

- 1 tablespoon of ground cinnamon
- 1 teaspoon of salt
- 2¼ cups of white sugar
- 1 cup of vegetable oil
- 3 cups of all-purpose flour
- 3 eggs
- 2 cups of zucchini, grated
- 1 cup of walnuts, chopped
- 3 teaspoons of vanilla extract
- 2 teaspoons of baking powder

DIRECTIONS

1. Strain together the baking powder, flour, cinnamon and salt in a bowl.
2. Whisk together the eggs, sugar, vanilla extract and vegetable oil in another bowl.
3. Sift in the baking powder mixture and fold in the walnuts and zucchini.
4. Grease 2 loaf pans and pour this mixture into them.
5. Place the loaf pans into the cooking tray.
6. Set the Air fryer to 325^{0}F for 20 minutes.
7. Insert the cooking tray in the Air fryer when it displays “Add Food”.
8. Remove from the oven when cooking time is complete.
9. Cut into preferred size slices and serve immediately.

20 MINUTES

16

Perfect Cheesy Eggs

BASIC RECIPE

10 MINUTES

12 MINUTES

2

DIRECTIONS

1. Cream together 1 egg, cream, salt, and black pepper in a bowl.
2. Line the pie pan with ham slices and pour in the egg mixture.
3. Crack the rest of the eggs on top and sprinkle with smoked paprika, salt, and black pepper.
4. Top evenly with chives and Parmesan cheese.
5. Place the pie pan in the cooking tray.
6. Set the Air fryer to 325ºF for 12 minutes.
7. Insert the cooking tray in the Air fryer when it displays "Add Food".
8. Remove from the oven when cooking time is complete and serve.

SHOPPING LIST

- 2-ounces of ham, sliced thinly
- 4 large eggs, divided
- 3 tablespoons of Parmesan cheese, grated
- finely
- 1/8 teaspoon of smoked paprika
- 2 teaspoons of fresh chives, minced
- 2 tablespoons of heavy cream
- 2 teaspoons of unsalted butter, softened
- Salt and black pepper, to taste

NUTRITION

Calories 356
Carbs 5.4g
Protein 24.9g
Fat 26.5g

Gourmet Cheesy Bread

BASIC RECIPE

10 MINUTES

15 MINUTES

2

DIRECTIONS

1. Place 2 cheese slices between the 2. and arrange the bread slices in the cooking tray.
2. Set the Air fryer to 355°F for 5 minutes.
Insert the cooking tray in the Air fryer
3. when it displays “Add Food”.
4. Remove from the oven when cooking time is complete.
5. Whisk thoroughly egg whites in a bowl and fold in the cheese, egg yolks, paprika, and mustard.
6. Spread this mixture over the bread slices and place it in the cooking tray.
7. Cook again in the Air fryer for about 10 minutes and dish out to serve

NUTRITION

Calories 164 Carbs 11.1g

Protein 10.2g Fat 9.2g

SHOPPING LIST

- 1 tablespoon of olives
- 1 tablespoon of mustard
- 1 tablespoon of paprika
- 3 bread slices
- 2 tablespoons of cheddar cheese
- 2 eggs, whites and yolks, separated
- 1 tablespoon of chives

Crust Less Quiche

INTERMEDIATE RECIPE

NUTRITION

Calories 348
Carbs 7.9g
Protein 26.1g
Fat 23.1g

DIRECTIONS

1. Combine all the ingredients into 2 greased ramekins and place them on the cooking tray.
2. Set the Air fryer to 340°F for 25 minutes. Insert the cooking tray in the Air fryer when it displays "Add Food".
3. Remove from the oven when cooking time is complete. Serve warm

SHOPPING LIST

- ½ cup of milk
- 1 cup of Gouda cheese, shredded
- 4 eggs
- ¼ cup of onion, chopped
- ½ cup of tomatoes, chopped
- Salt, to taste

6

2 MINUTES

25 MINUTES

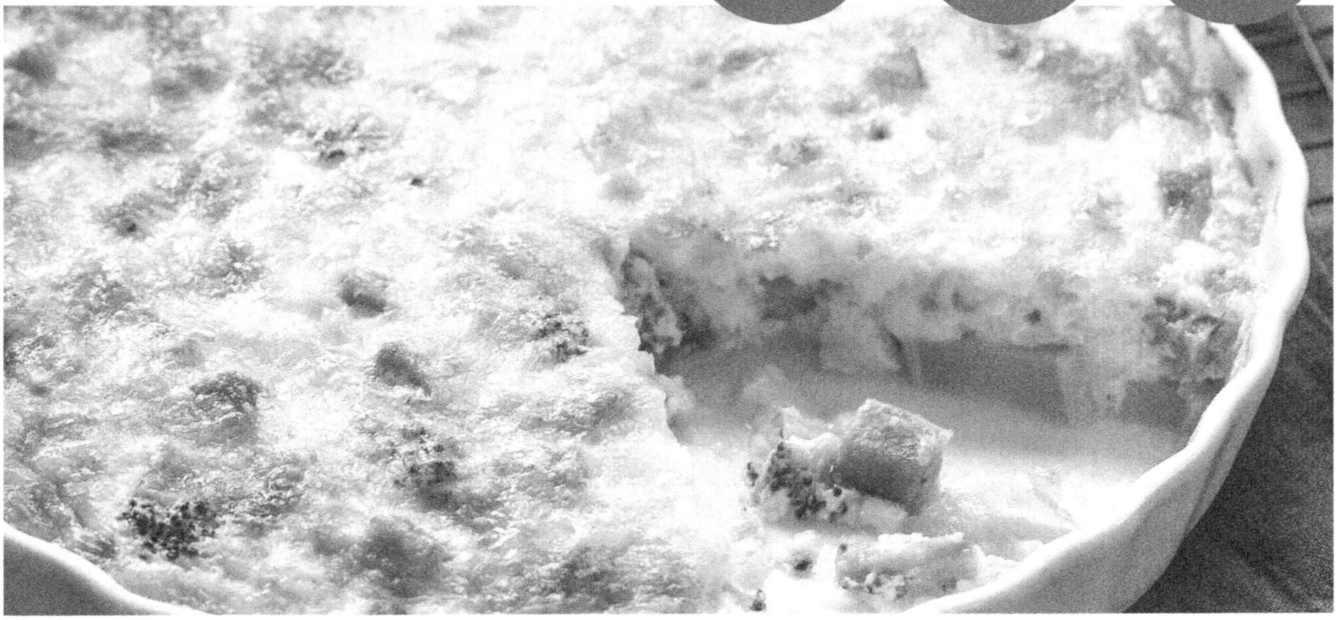

Breakfast Creamy Donuts

INTERMEDIATE RECIPES

NUTRITION

Calories 303
Protein 4.8g
Carbs 49.1g
Fat 10.2g

DIRECTIONS

1. Cream together sugar, egg yolks, and butter in a bowl.
2. Strain together flour, baking powder, baking soda and salt in another bowl.
3. Fold in the creamed sugar mixture and sour cream to form a dough.
4. Slice the dough in half and roll into a 2-inch thickness.
5. Drizzle melted butter over both sides of the dough and move in the cooking tray.
6. Set the Air fryer to 365⁰F for 8 minutes. Insert the cooking tray in the Air fryer when it displays "Add Food".
7. Remove from the oven when cooking time is complete.
8. Serve sprinkled with cinnamon and caster sugar.

SHOPPING LIST

- 3 medium red bell peppers, remove and
- discard seeds, slice into quarters
- Nonstick cooking spray
- 1 medium onion, sliced into 1/2-inch slices
- 1½ teaspoons of baking powder
- 1 pinch of baking soda
- 1/3 cup of caster sugar
- 1 teaspoon of cinnamon
- ½ cup of sugar
- 4 tablespoons of butter, softened and divided
- 2 large egg yolks
- 2¼ cups of plain flour
- 1 teaspoon salt
- ½ cup of sour cream

10 MINUTES

8 MINUTES

8

Mixed Scrambled Eggs

BASIC RECIPE

NUTRITION

Calories 351
Protein 26.4g
Carbs 25.2g
Fat 22g

SHOPPING LIST

- 8 grape tomatoes, halved
- ½ cup of Parmesan cheese, grated
- ¾ cup of milk
- 1 tablespoon of butter
- Salt and black pepper, to taste
- 4 eggs

DIRECTIONS

1. Whip the eggs with milk, salt, and black pepper in a bowl.
2. Pour the egg mixture into the cooking tray along with the grape tomatoes and cheese.
3. Set the Air fryer to 360 degrees F for 10 minutes.
4. Insert the cooking tray in the Air fryer when it displays "Add Food".
5. Remove from the oven when cooking time is complete. Serve warm.

Coconut Shrimp

BASIC RECIPE

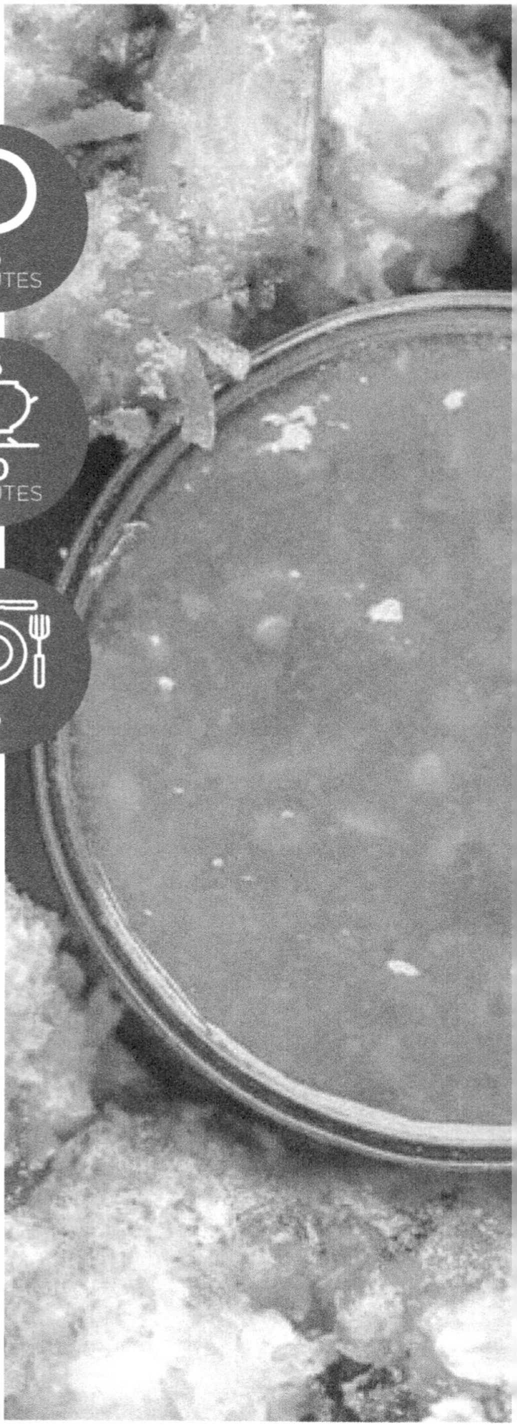

NUTRITION

Calories 213
Fat 8g
Protein 15g
Sugar 3g

SHOPPING LIST

- 1 C. almond flour
- 1 C. panko breadcrumbs
- 1 tablespoon coconut flour
- 1 C. unsweetened, dried coconut
- 1 egg white
- 12 raw large shrimp

DIRECTIONS

1. Put shrimp on paper towels to drain.
2. Mix in the coconut and panko breadcrumbs.
3. Then mix in coconut flour and almond flour in a different bowl.
4. Set aside.
5. Dip shrimp into the flour mixture, then into egg white, and then into the coconut mixture.
6. Place in the air fryer basket. Repeat with remaining shrimp.
7. Set temperature to 350°F, and set time to 10 minutes.
8. Turn halfway through the cooking process.

Grilled Salmon

BASIC RECIPE

5 MINUTES

10 MINUTES

3

SHOPPING LIST

- 2 salmon fillets
- 1/2 tsp lemon pepper
- 1/2 tsp garlic powder
- salt
- 1/3 cup soy sauce
- 1/3 cup sugar
- 1 tbsp olive oil
- lemon wedges for gamish

NUTRITION

Calories 312	Protein 19g
Fat 11g	Sugar 5g

DIRECTIONS

1. Season the salmon fillets with lemon pepper, garlic powder and salt.
2. In a shallow bowl, add a third cup of water and combine the olive oil, soy sauce and sugar.
3. Place salmon in the bowl and immerse in the sauce.
4. Cover with cling film and allow to marinate in the refrigerator for at least an hour.
5. Preheat the Air Fryer to 350^{0}F
6. Place salmon into the air fryer and cook for 10 minutes or more until the fish is tender.
7. Serve with lemon wedges

Bacon Wrapped Shrimp

INTERMEDIATE RECIPE

SHOPPING LIST

- 1¼ pound tiger shrimp, peeled and deveined
- 1 pound bacon

5 MINUTES

5 MINUTES

4

DIRECTIONS

1. Wrap each shrimp with a slice of bacon.
2. Refrigerate for about 20 minutes. Preheat the
3. Air Fryer to 390⁰F.
4. Arrange the
5. shrimp in the air fryer basket. Cook for about 5-7 minutes.

NUTRITION

Calories 202
Fat 7g
Protein 3g
Sugar 2g

Crispy Paprika Fish Fillets

BASIC RECIPE

SHOPPING LIST

- 1/2 cup seasoned breadcrumbs
- 1 tablespoon balsamic vinegar
- 1/2 teaspoon seasoned salt
- 1 teaspoon paprika
- 1/2 teaspoon ground black pepper
- 1 teaspoon celery seed
- 2 fish fillets, halved
- 1 egg, beaten

NUTRITION

Calories 196
Fat 6g
Protein 3.3g
Sugar 3g

5 MINUTES

15 MINUTES

4

DIRECTIONS

1. Add the breadcrumbs, vinegar, salt, paprika, ground black pepper, and celery seeds to your food processor.
2. Process for about 30 seconds.
3. Coat the fish fillets with the beaten egg; then, coat them with the breadcrumbs mixture.
4. Pour into the rack/basket. Place the Rack on the middle-shelf of the Air Fryer.
5. Set temperature to 350°F, and set time to 15 minutes.

Air Fryer Salmon

BASIC RECIPE

NUTRITION

Calories 185

Fat 11g

Protein 21g

5 MINUTES

SHOPPING LIST

- ½ teaspoon salt
- ½ teaspoon garlic powder
- ½ teaspoon smoked paprika
- Salmon

DIRECTIONS

1. Mix spices and sprinkle onto salmon.
2. Place seasoned salmon in the Air Fryer.
3. Pour into the rack/basket.
4. Place the rack on the middle-shelf of the Air Fryer.
5. Set temperature to 400°F, and set time to 10 minutes.

10 MINUTES

2

Steamed Salmon & Sauce

BASIC RECIPE

NUTRITION

Calories 172
Protein 13g
Fat 7g
Sugar 2g

DIRECTIONS

1. Pour the water into the tray of the Air Fryer and start heating to 285°F.
2. Drizzle oil over the fish and spread it.
3. Salt the fish to taste.
4. Now pop it into the Air Fryer for 10 minutes. In the meantime, mix the yogurt, cream, dill and a bit of salt to make the sauce.
5. When the fish is done, serve with the sauce and garnish with sprigs of dill.

SHOPPING LIST

- 1 cup of water
- 2 x 6 oz. fresh salmon
- 2 teaspoon vegetable oil
- ½ cup plain greek yogurt
- ½ cup sour cream
- 2 tablespoon finely chopped dill (keep a bit for garnishing)
- a pinch of salt to taste

5 MINUTES

10 MINUTES

2

Sweet & Savory Breaded Shrimp

BASIC RECIPE

NUTRITION

Calories 143 | Protein 10.3g
Fat 5g | Sugar 1.9g

5 MINUTES | 20 MINUTES | 2

SHOPPING LIST

- ½ pound of fresh shrimp, peeled from their
- shells and rinsed
- 2 raw eggs
- ½ cup of breadcrumbs (we like Panko, but
- any brand or home recipe will do)
- ½ white onion, peeled and rinsed and finely
- chopped
- 1 teaspoon of ginger-garlic paste
- ½ teaspoon of turmeric powder
- ½ teaspoon of red chili powder
- ½ teaspoon of cumin powder
- ½ teaspoon of black pepper powder
- ½ teaspoon of dry mango powder
- Pinch of salt

DIRECTIONS

1. Cover the air fryer's basket with a lining of tin foil, leaving the edges uncovered to allow air to circulate through the basket.
2. Preheat the Air Fryer to 350⁰F.
3. In a large mixing bowl, beat the eggs until fluffy until the yolks and whites are fully combined.
4. Dunk all the shrimp in the egg mixture, fully submerging.
5. In a separate mixing bowl, combine the bread crumbs with all the dry ingredients until evenly blended.
6. One by one, coat the egg-covered shrimp in the mixed dry ingredients so that fully covered, and place on the foil-lined air-fryer basket.
7. Set the Air Fryer timer to 20 minutes.
8. Halfway through the cooking time, shake the handle of the air-fryer so that the breaded shrimp jostles inside and fry-coverage is even.
9. After 20 minutes, when the fryer shuts off, the shrimp will be perfectly cooked and their breaded crust golden-brown and delicious!
10. Using tongs, remove from the air fryer and place in a serving dish to

cool. coat the egg-covered shrimp in the mixed dry ingredients so that fully covered, and place on the foil-lined air-fryer basket.

11. Set the Air Fryer timer to 20 minutes.
12. Halfway through the cooking time, shake the handle of the air-fryer so that the breaded shrimp jostles inside and fry-coverage is even.
13. After 20 minutes, when the fryer shuts off, the shrimp will be perfectly cooked and their breaded crust golden-brown and delicious! Using tongs, remove from the air fryer and set on a serving dish to cool.

Indian Fish Fingers

INTERMEDIATE RECIPE

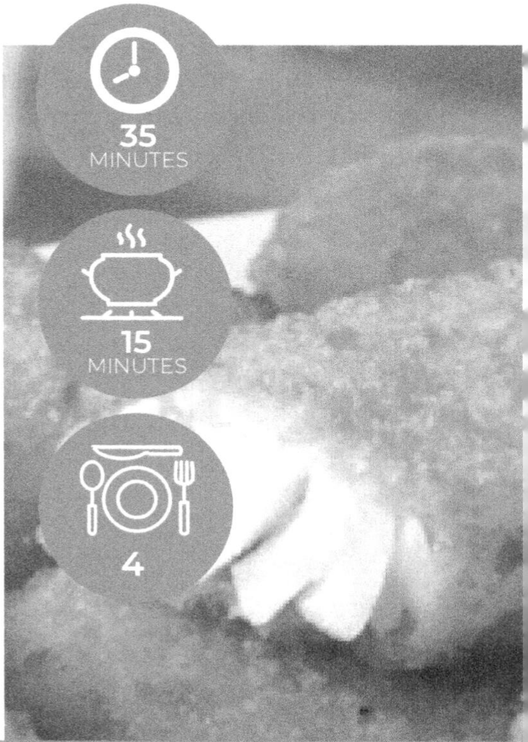

DIRECTIONS

1. Start by removing any skin on the fish, washing, and patting dry.
2. Cut the fish into fingers.
3. In a medium bowl mix all ingredients except for fish, mint, and bread crumbs.
4. Bury the fingers in the mixture and refrigerate for 30 minutes.
5. Remove from the bowl from the fridge and mix in mint leaves. In a separate bowl beat the egg, pour bread crumbs into a third bowl.
6. Dip the fingers in the egg bowl then toss them in the bread crumbs bowl.
7. Pour into the Oven rack/basket. Place the Rack on the middle-shelf of the Air Fryer.
8. Set temperature to 360°F, and set time to 15 minutes, toss the fingers halfway through.

SHOPPING LIST

- 1/2 pound fish fillet
- 1 tablespoon finely chopped fresh mint
- leaves or any fresh herbs
- 1/3 cup bread crumbs
- 1 teaspoon ginger garlic paste or ginger and
- garlic powders
- 1 hot green chili finely chopped
- 1/2 teaspoon paprika
- Generous pinch of black pepper
- Salt to taste
- 3/4 tablespoons lemon juice
- 3/4 teaspoons garam masala powder
- 1/3 teaspoon rosemary
- 1 egg

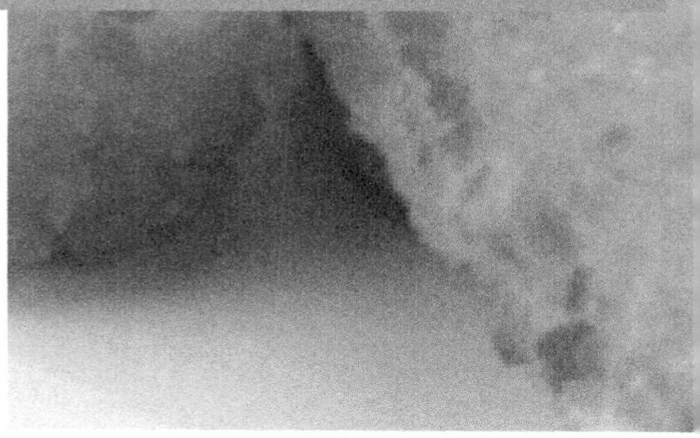

NUTRITION

Calories 187
Fat 7g
Protein 11g
Fiber 1g

Healthy Fish & Chips

BASIC RECIPE

DIRECTIONS

1. Add almond flour to one bowl, beat egg in another bowl, and add panko breadcrumbs to the third bowl, mixed with Old Bay seasoning.
2. Dredge tilapia in flour, then egg, and then breadcrumbs.
3. Place coated fish in Smart Air Fryer Oven along with fries.
4. Set temperature to 390°F, and set time to 15 minutes.

5 MINUTES

15 MINUTES

3

SHOPPING LIST

- Old Bay seasoning
- ½ C. panko breadcrumbs
- 1 egg
- 2 tablespoon almond flour
- 4-6 ounce tilapia fillets
- Frozen crinkle cut fries

NUTRITION

Calories 219

Fat 5g

Protein 25g

Sugar 1g

Quick Paella

BASIC RECIPE

NUTRITION

Calories 345
Protein 18g
Fat 1g
Fiber 4g

DIRECTIONS

1. In a 6-by-6-by-2-inch pan, combine the rice, artichoke hearts, vegetable broth, turmeric, and thyme, and stir gently.
2. Place in the Smart Air Fryer Oven and bake for 8 to 9 minutes or until the rice is hot.
3. Remove from the air fryer and gently stir in the shrimp, peas, and tomato.
4. Cook for 5 to 8 minutes or until the shrimp and peas are hot and the paella is bubbling.

SHOPPING LIST

- 1 (10-ounce) package frozen cooked rice,
- thawed
- 1 (6-ounce) jar artichoke hearts, drained and
- chopped
- ¼ cup vegetable broth
- ½ teaspoon turmeric
- ½ teaspoon dried thyme
- 1 cup frozen cooked small shrimp
- ½ cup frozen baby peas
- 1 tomato, diced

4

7 MINUTES

15 MINUTES

Air Fryer Catfish

BASIC RECIPES

NUTRITION

Calories 208
Protein 17g
Fat 5g
Sugar 0.5g

5 MINUTES

13 MINUTES

4

DIRECTIONS

1. Ensure your Air Fryer is preheated to 400 degrees.
2. Rinse off catfish fillets and pat dry. Add fish fry seasoning to Ziploc baggie, then catfish.
3. Shake the bag and ensure the fish gets well coated.
4. Spray each fillet with olive oil. Add fillets to the air fryer basket.
5. Set temperature to 400°F, and set time to 10 minutes.
6. Cook 10 minutes.
7. Then flip and cook for another 2-3 minutes. Garnish with parsley then serve

SHOPPING LIST

- 1 tablespoon chopped parsley
- 1 tablespoon olive oil
- ¼ C. seasoned fish fry
- 4 catfish fillets

Tuna Veggie Stir-Fry

BASIC RECIPE

NUTRITION

Calories 187
Protein 17g
Fat 8g
Fiber 2g

SHOPPING LIST

- 1 tablespoon olive oil
- 1 red bell pepper, chopped
- 1 cup green beans, cut into 2-inch pieces
- 1 onion, sliced
- 2 cloves garlic, sliced
- 2 tablespoons low-sodium soy sauce
- 1 tablespoon honey
- ½ pound fresh tuna, cubed
- salt and pepper

DIRECTIONS

1. In a 6-inch metal bowl, combine the olive oil, pepper, green beans, onion, and garlic.
2. Pour into the Oven rack/basket.
3. Place the Rack on the middle-shelf of the Air Fryer.
4. Set temperature to 350°F, and set time to 4 to 6 minutes, stirring once, until crisp and tender.
5. Add soy sauce, honey, and tuna, and stir.
6. Cook for another 3 to 6 minutes, stirring once until the tuna is cooked as desired.
7. Tuna can be served rare or medium-rare, or you can cook it until well done.

5 MINUTES

12 MINUTES

4

Salmon Quiche

INTERMEDIATE RECIPE

NUTRITION

Calories 203
Fat 10g
Protein 19.3g
Fiber 5g

SHOPPING LIST

- 5 oz. salmon fillet
- 1/2 tablespoon lemon juice
- 1/2 cup flour
- 1/4 cup butter, melted
- 2 eggs and 1 egg yolk
- 3 tbsps. whipped cream
- 1 tsp mustard
- Black pepper to taste
- Salt and pepper
- *Quiche pan

DIRECTIONS

1. Clean and cut the salmon into small cubes.
2. Heat the Smart Air Fryer Oven to 375^{0}F
3. Pour the lemon juice over the salmon cubes and allow to marinate for an hour.
4. Combine a tablespoon of water with the butter, flour and yolk in a large bowl.
5. With your hands, knead the mixture until smooth
6. On a clean surface, use a rolling pin to form a circle of dough. Scoop this into the quiche pan, using your fingers to adhere the pastry to the edges
7. Whisk the cream, mustard and eggs together.
8. Season with salt and pepper. Add the marinated salmon into the bowl and combine.
9. Pour the content of the bowl into the dough lined quiche pan
10. Put the pan in the Smart Air Fryer Oven tray and cook for 25 minutes until browned and crispy.

5 MINUTES

12 MINUTES

4

Tuna Patties

BASIC RECIPE

SHOPPING LIST

- 2 (6-ounce) cans water-packed plain tuna
- 2 teaspoons Dijon mustard
- ½ cup breadcrumbs
- 1 tablespoon fresh lime juice
- 2 tablespoons fresh parsley, chopped
- 1 egg
- Air fryer of hot sauce
- 3 tablespoons canola oil
- Salt and freshly ground black pepper, to taste

10 MINUTES

10 MINUTES

4

NUTRITION

Calories 203
Fat 4.7g
Protein 22g
Fiber 3g

DIRECTIONS

1. Drain most of the liquid from the canned tuna.
2. In a bowl, add the fish, mustard, crumbs, citrus juice, parsley and hot sauce and mix till well combined.
3. Add a little canola oil if it seems too dry.
4. Add egg, salt and stir to combine.
5. Make the patties from the tuna mixture. Refrigerate the tuna patties for about 2 hours.
6. Pour into the Oven rack/basket. Place the Rack on the middle-shelf of the Smart Air Fryer Oven.
7. Set temperature to 355°F, and set time to 12 minutes.

Bang Panko Breaded Fried Shrimp

BASIC RECIPE

SHOPPING LIST

- 1 teaspoon paprika
- Montreal chicken seasoning
- ¾ cup panko bread crumbs
- ½ cup almond flour
- 1 egg white
- 1 pound raw shrimp (peeled and deveined)
- Bang Bang Sauce:
- ¼ cup sweet chili sauce
- 2 tablespoon sriracha sauce
- 1/3 cup plain Greek yogurt

DIRECTIONS

1. Ensure your Air Fryer is preheated to 400°F.
2. Season all shrimp with seasonings.
3. Add flour to one bowl, egg white in another, and breadcrumbs to a third.
4. Dip seasoned shrimp in flour, then egg whites, and then breadcrumbs.
5. Spray coated shrimp with olive oil and add to air fryer basket.
6. Set temperature to 400°F, and set time to 4 minutes. Cook 4 minutes, flip, and cook an additional 4 minutes.
7. To make the sauce, mix all sauce ingredients until smooth.

NUTRITION

Calories 212
Carbs 12g
Fat 1g
Protein 37g
Sugar 0.5g

5 MINUTES

8 MINUTES

4

Cornish Game Hens

INTERMEDIATE RECIPE

SHOPPING LIST

- ½ cup olive oil
- 1 teaspoon fresh rosemary, chopped
- 1 teaspoon fresh thyme, chopped
- 1 teaspoon fresh lemon zest, finely grated
- ¼ teaspoon sugar
- ¼ teaspoon red pepper flakes, crushed
- Salt and ground black pepper, as required
- 2 pounds Cornish game hen, backbone
- removed and halved

NUTRITION

Calories 523
Carbs 0.8g
Protein 52.9g
Fat 34.1g
Sugar 0.6g
Sodium 143mg

20 MINUTES

16 MINUTES

4

DIRECTIONS

1. In a bowl, mix oil, herbs, lemon zest, sugar, and spices.
2. Add the hen portions and generously coat with the marinade.
3. Cover and refrigerate for about 24 hours.
4. In a strainer, place the hen portions and set them aside to drain any liquid.
5. Set the temperature of the Air Fryer to 390°F. Grease an Air Fryer basket.
6. Place hen portions into the prepared Air fryer basket.
7. Air Fry for about 14-16 minutes.
8. Remove from the Air Fryer and transfer the hen portions onto serving plates and serve.

Roasted Chicken with Potatoes

INTERMEDIATE RECIPE

NUTRITION

Calories 431
Fat 16.2g
Carbs 178g
Sugar 1.3g
Protein 511g
Sodium 153mg

15 MINUTES

SHOPPING LIST

- 1 (1½-pounds) whole chicken
- Salt and ground black pepper, as required
- 1 tablespoon olive oil
- ½ pound small potatoes

60 MINUTES

2

DIRECTIONS

1. Set the temperature of the Air Fryer to 390°F.
2. Grease an Air Fryer basket. Season the chicken with salt and black pepper.
3. Place chicken into the prepared Air Fryer basket.
4. Air Fry for about 35-40 minutes or until done completely.
5. Transfer the chicken onto a platter and cover with a piece of foil to keep warm.
6. In a bowl, add the potatoes, oil, salt, and black pepper and toss to coat well.
7. Again, set the temperature of the Air Fryer to 390°F. Grease an Air Fryer basket.
8. Place potatoes into the prepared Air Fryer basket.
9. Air Fry for about 20 minutes or until golden brown. Remove from the Air Fryer and transfer potatoes into a bowl.
10. Cut the chicken into desired size pieces using a sharp knife and serve alongside the potatoes.

Herbed Roasted Chicken

INTERMEDIATE RECIPE

NUTRITION

Calories 860
Carbs 1.3g
Protein 71.1g
Fat 50g
Sugar 0.2g
Sodium 299mg

SHOPPING LIST

- 3 garlic cloves, minced
- 1 teaspoon fresh lemon zest, finely grated
- 1 teaspoon dried thyme, crushed
- 1 teaspoon dried oregano, crushed
- 1 teaspoon dried rosemary, crushed
- 1 teaspoon smoked paprika
- Salt and ground black pepper, as required
- 2 tablespoons fresh lemon juice
- 2 tablespoons olive oil
- 1 (5-pounds) whole chicken

DIRECTIONS

1. In a bowl, mix the garlic, lemon zest, herbs and spices.
2. Rub the chicken evenly with herb mixture.
3. Drizzle the chicken with lemon juice and oil.
4. Set aside at room temperature for about 2 hours.
5. Set the temperature of the Air Fryer to 360°F. Grease an Air Fryer basket.
6. Place chicken into the prepared Air Fryer basket, breast side down. Air Fry for about 50 minutes.
7. Flip the chicken and Air Fry for about 10 more minutes. Remove from the Air Fryer and place chicken onto a cutting board for about 10 minutes before carving.
8. With a knife, slice the chicken into desired size pieces and serve.

15 MINUTES

60 MINUTES

7

Spiced Roasted Chicken

INTERMEDIATE RECIPE

NUTRITION

Calories 871
Carbs 1.7g
Protein 70.6g
Fat 60g
Sugar 0.4g
Sodium 296mg

15 MINUTES

SHOPPING LIST

- 2 teaspoons dried thyme
- 2 teaspoons paprika
- 1 teaspoon cayenne pepper
- 1 teaspoon ground white pepper
- 1 teaspoon onion powder
- 1 teaspoon garlic powder
- Salt and ground black pepper, as required
- 3 tablespoons oil
- 1 (5-pounds) whole chicken, necks and giblets removed

DIRECTIONS

1. In a bowl, mix the thyme and spices.
2. Generously, coat the chicken with oil and then rub it with a spice mixture.
3. Set the temperature of the Air Fryer to 350°F. Grease an Air Fryer basket.
4. Place chicken into the prepared Air Fryer basket, breast side down.
5. Air Fry for about 30 minutes.
6. Flip the chicken and Air Fry for about 30 more minutes.
7. Remove from the Air Fryer and place chicken onto a cutting board for about 10 minutes before carving.
8. Slice the chicken into desired size pieces using a sharp knife and serve.

60 MINUTES

6

Spicy Chicken Legs

BASIC RECIPE

DIRECTIONS

1. In a bowl, put the chicken legs, and buttermilk. Refrigerate for about 2 hours.
2. In another bowl, mix the flour and spices.
3. Remove the chicken from buttermilk.
4. Coat the chicken legs with flour mixture, then dip into buttermilk and finally, coat with the flour mixture again.
5. Set the temperature of the Air Fryer to 360°F.
6. Grease an Air Fryer basket. Arrange chicken legs into the prepared Air Fryer basket and drizzle with the oil Air Fry for about 20-25 minutes.
7. Remove from the Air Fryer and transfer chicken legs onto a serving platter.
8. Serve hot.

NUTRITION

Calories 781	Protein 55.9g	Sugar 4.7g
Carbs 69.5g	Fat 7.6g	Sodium 288mg

SHOPPING LIST

- 3 (8-ounces) chicken legs
- 1 cup buttermilk
- 2 cups white flour
- 1 teaspoon garlic powder
- 1 teaspoon onion powder
- 1 teaspoon ground cumin
- 1 teaspoon paprika
- Salt and ground black pepper, as required
- 1 tablespoon olive oil

Tandoori Chicken Legs

INTERMEDIATE RECIPE

15 MINUTES | 20 MINUTES | 4

DIRECTIONS

1. In a bowl, mix well chicken legs, lemon juice, ginger paste, garlic paste, and salt.
2. Set aside for about 15 minutes.
3. Meanwhile, in another bowl, mix the curd, spices, and food color.
4. Add the chicken legs into the bowl and generously coat with the spice mixture.
5. Cover the bowl of chicken and refrigerate for at least 10-12 hours.
6. Set the temperature of the air fryer to 445°F.
7. Line an air fryer basket with a piece of foil. Arrange chicken legs into the prepared air fryer basket.
8. Air fry for about 18-20 minutes.
9. Remove from air fryer and transfer the chicken legs onto serving plates.

NUTRITION

Calories 356	Protein 51.5g	Sugar 0.5g
Carbs 3.7g	Fat 13.9g	Sodium 259mg

SHOPPING LIST

- 4 chicken legs
- 3 tablespoons fresh lemon juice
- 3 teaspoons ginger paste
- 3 teaspoons garlic paste
- Salt, as required
- 4 tablespoons hung curd*
- 2 tablespoons tandoori masala powder
- 2 teaspoons red chili powder
- 1 teaspoon garam masala powder
- 1 teaspoon ground cumin
- 1 teaspoon ground coriander
- 1 teaspoon ground turmeric
- Ground black pepper, as required
- Pinch of orange food color

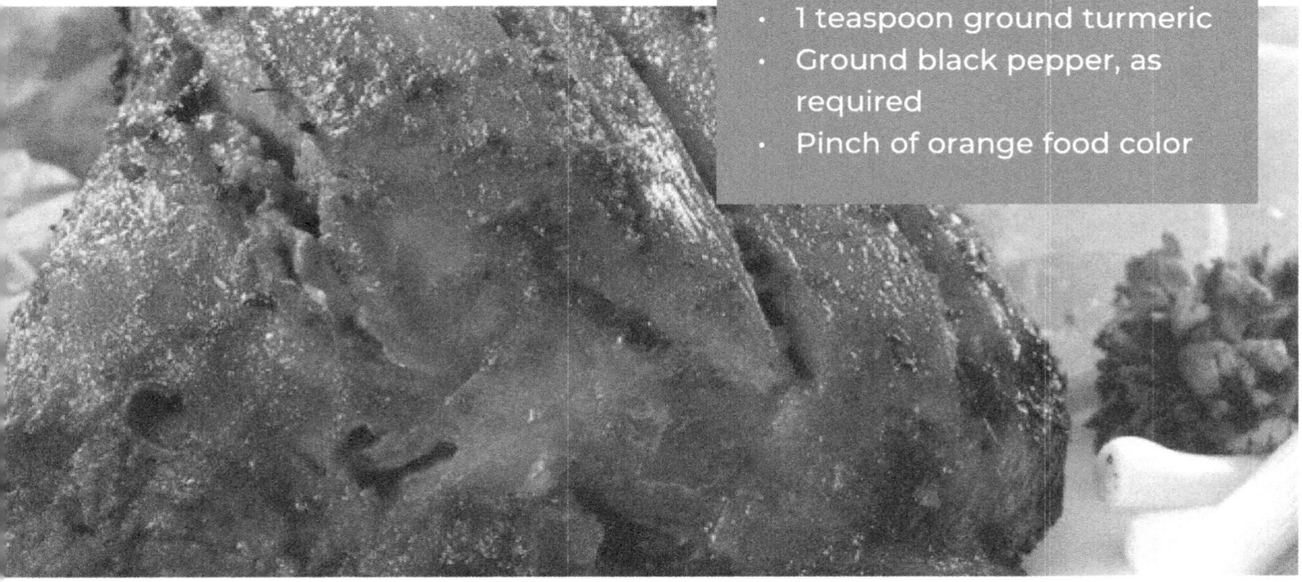

Gingered Chicken Drumsticks

BASIC RECIPE

NUTRITION

Calories 338	Protein 47.4g	Sugar 0.4g
Carbs 2.6g	Fat 13.9g	Sodium 192mg

SHOPPING LIST

- ¼ cup full-fat coconut milk
- 2 teaspoons fresh ginger, minced
- 2 teaspoons galangal, minced
- 2 teaspoons ground turmeric
- Salt, to taste
- 3 (6-ounces) chicken drumsticks

DIRECTIONS

1. In a bowl, mix the coconut milk, galangal, ginger, and spices.
2. Add the chicken drumsticks and generously coat with the marinade.
3. Refrigerate to marinate for at least 6-8 hours.
4. Set the temperature of the Air Fryer to 375°F.
5. Grease an Air Fryer basket. Place chicken drumsticks into the prepared Air Fryer basket in a single layer.
6. Air Fry for about 20-25 minutes. Remove from Air Fryer and transfer the chicken drumsticks onto a serving platter.
7. Serve hot.

3

10 MINUTES

25 MINUTES

Sweet & Spicy Chicken Drumsticks

BASIC RECIPES

NUTRITION

Calories 341 Protein 47.7g Sugar 1.8g
Carbs 3.3g Fat 14.1g Sodium 182mg

15 MINUTES
20 MINUTES
4

DIRECTIONS

1. In a bowl, mix garlic, mustard, brown sugar, oil, and spices. Rub the chicken drumsticks with marinade and refrigerate to marinate for about 20-30 minutes.
2. Set the temperature of the Air Fryer to 390°F. Grease an Air Fryer basket.
3. Arrange drumsticks into the prepared Air Fryer basket in a single layer.
4. Air Fry for about 10 minutes and then 10 more minutes at 300°F.
5. Remove from Air Fryer and transfer the chicken drumsticks onto a serving platter.
6. Serve hot.

SHOPPING LIST

- 1 garlic clove, crushed
- 1 tablespoon mustard
- 2 teaspoons brown sugar
- 1 teaspoon cayenne pepper
- 1 teaspoon red chili powder
- Salt and ground black pepper, as required
- 1 tablespoon vegetable oil
- 4 (6-ounces) chicken drumsticks

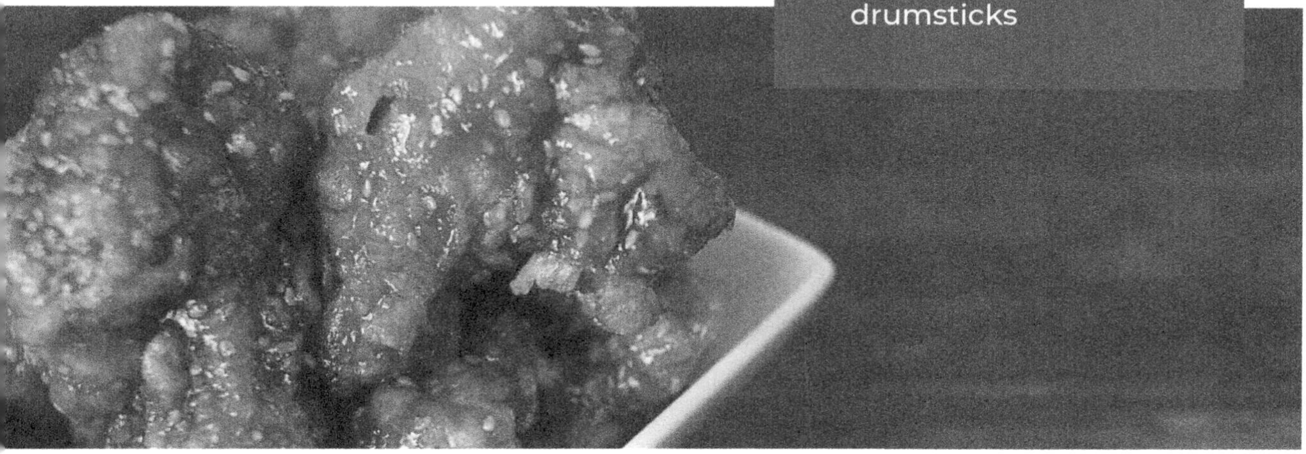

Honey Glazed Chicken Drumsticks

BASIC RECIPE

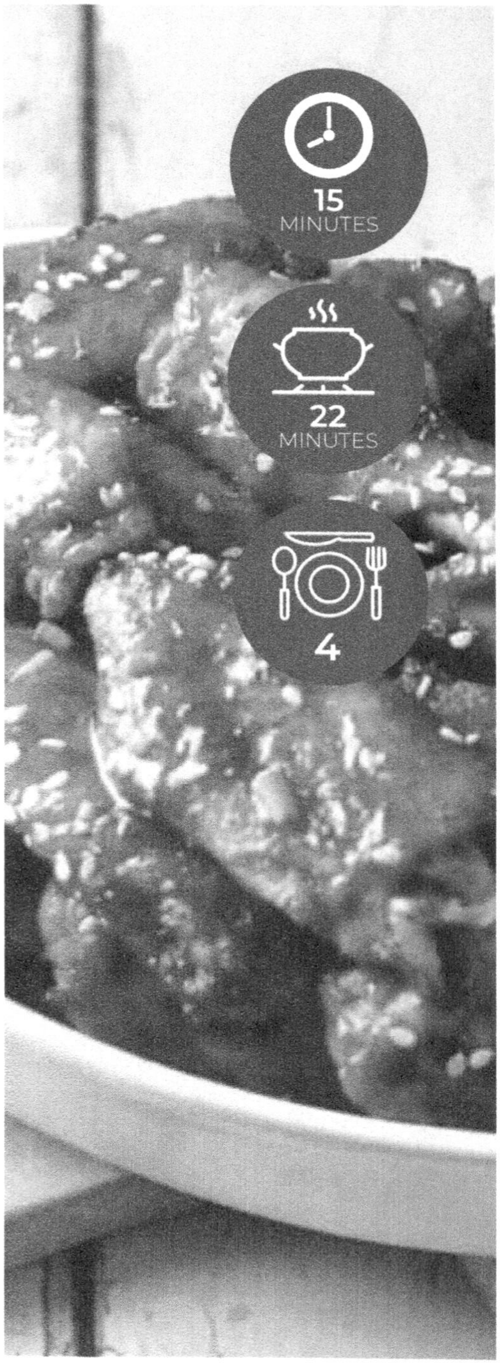

NUTRITION

Calories 377 | Protein 47.6g | Sugar 4.5g
Carbs 5.9g | Fat 3.6g | Sodium 353mg

SHOPPING LIST

- ¼ cup Dijon mustard
- 1 tablespoon honey
- 2 tablespoons olive oil
- ½ tablespoon fresh rosemary, minced
- 1 tablespoon fresh thyme, minced
- Salt and ground black pepper, as required
- 4 (6-ounces) boneless chicken drumsticks

DIRECTIONS

1. In a bowl, mix well the mustard, honey, oil, herbs, salt, and black pepper.
2. Add the drumsticks and generously coat with the mixture. Cover and refrigerate to marinate overnight.
3. Set the temperature of the Air Fryer to 320°F. Grease an Air Fryer basket.
4. Arrange the chicken drumsticks into the prepared Air Fryer basket in a single layer.
5. Air Fry for about 12 minutes. Now, set the temperature of the Air Fryer to 355°F.
6. Air Fry for 5-10 more minutes. Remove from Air Fryer and transfer the chicken drumsticks onto a serving platter.
7. Serve hot.

Chinese Chicken Drumsticks

BASIC RECIPE

NUTRITION

Calories 400
Carbs 22.7g
Protein 48.9g
Fat 11.4g
Sugar 0.2g
Sodium 279mg

SHOPPING LIST

- 1 tablespoon oyster sauce
- 1 teaspoon light soy sauce
- ½ teaspoon sesame oil
- 1 teaspoon Chinese five-spice powder
- Salt and ground white pepper, as required
- 4 (6-ounces) chicken drumsticks
- 1 cup cornflour

DIRECTIONS

In a bowl, mix the sauces, oil, five-spice powder, salt, and black pepper. Add the chicken drumsticks and generously coat with the marinade.

Refrigerate for at least 30-40 minutes.

In a shallow dish, place the cornflour.

Remove the chicken from marinade and lightly coat it with cornflour.

5. Set the temperature of the Air Fryer to
6. 390° F. Grease an Air Fryer basket. Arrange chicken drumsticks into the prepared Air Fryer basket in a single
7. Air fry for about 20 minutes. Remove from Air Fryer and transfer the chicken drumsticks onto a serving platter. Serve hot.

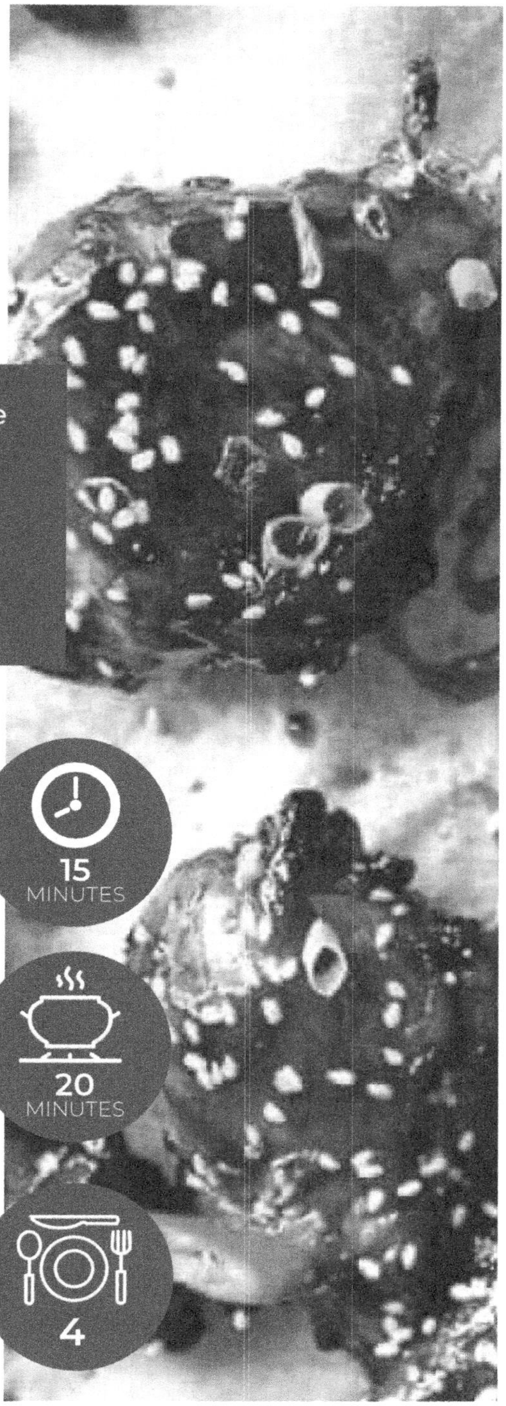

Crispy Chicken Drumsticks

BASIC RECIPE

SHOPPING LIST

- 4 (4-ounces) chicken drumsticks
- ½ cup buttermilk
- ½ cup all-purpose flour
- ½ cup panko breadcrumbs
- ¼ teaspoon baking powder
- ¼ teaspoon dried oregano
- ¼ teaspoon dried thyme
- ¼ teaspoon celery salt
- ¼ teaspoon garlic powder
- ¼ teaspoon ground ginger
- ¼ teaspoon cayenne pepper
- ¼ teaspoon paprika
- Salt and ground black pepper, as required
- 3 tablespoons butter, melted

NUTRITION

Calories 771
Carbs 32.1g
Protein 68.7g
Fat 33.1g
Sugar 3.2g
Sodium 449mg

15 MINUTES

20 MINUTES

2

DIRECTIONS

1. Place the chicken drumsticks and buttermilk in a resealable plastic bag.
2. Squeeze the air out and seal the bag tightly.
3. Refrigerate for about 2-3 hours.
4. In a shallow bowl, mix flour, breadcrumbs, baking powder, herbs, and spices.
5. Remove the chicken drumsticks from a bag and shake off the excess buttermilk.
6. Coat chicken drumsticks evenly with the seasoned flour mixture.
7. Set the temperature of the air fryer to 390°F. Line an air fryer basket with a piece of foil.
8. Arrange chicken drumsticks into the prepared air fryer basket.
9. Air fry for about 20 minutes, flipping once and coating with the melted butter.
10. Remove from the air fryer and transfer the chicken drumsticks onto serving plates.
11. Serve hot.

Sweet & Sour Chicken Thighs

BASIC RECIPE

SHOPPING LIST

- 1 scallion, finely chopped
- 1 garlic clove, minced
- ½ tablespoon soy sauce
- ½ tablespoon rice vinegar
- 1 teaspoon sugar
- Salt and ground black pepper, as required
- 2 (4-ounces) skinless, boneless chicken thighs
- ½ cup corn flour

DIRECTIONS

1. Mix all the ingredients except chicken, and corn flour in a bowl.
2. Add the chicken thighs and generously coat with marinade.
3. Add the corn-flour to another bowl.
4. Remove the chicken thighs from marinade and coat with corn flour.
5. Set the temperature of Air Fryer to 390°F.
6. Grease an Air Fryer basket. Arrange chicken thighs into the prepared Air Fryer basket, skin side down.
7. Air Fry for about 10 minutes and then another 10 minutes at 355°F.
8. Remove from Air Fryer and transfer the chicken thighs onto a serving platter. Serve hot.

10 MINUTES

20 MINUTES

2

NUTRITION

Calories 264	Fat 5.2g
Carbs 25.3g	Sugar 2.8g
Protein 27.8g	Sodium 347mg

Crispy Chicken Thighs

BASIC RECIPE

NUTRITION

Calories 353
Carbs 12g
Protein 31.5g
Fat 18.8g
Sugar 0.1g
Sodium 749mg

SHOPPING LIST

- ½ cup all-purpose flour
- 1½ tablespoons Cajun seasoning
- 1 teaspoon seasoning salt
- 1 egg
- 4 (4-ounces) skin-on chicken thighs

DIRECTIONS

1. Mix the flour, Cajun seasoning, and salt in a shallow bowl.
2. In another bowl, crack the egg and beat well.
3. Coat each chicken thigh with the flour mixture, then dip into beaten egg and finally, coat with the flour mixture again.
4. Shake off the excess flour thoroughly.
5. Set the temperature of the Air Fryer to 390°F.
6. Grease an Air Fryer basket. Arrange chicken thighs into the prepared Air Fryer basket, skin side down.
7. Air Fry for about 25 minutes.
8. Remove from Air Fryer and transfer the chicken thighs onto a serving platter.
9. Serve hot.

15 MINUTES

25 MINUTES

4

Cheesy Chicken Cutlets

BASIC RECIPE

NUTRITION

Calories 503
Carbs 42g
Protein 49.3g
Fat 42.3g
Sugar 1.3g
Sodium 226mg

15 MINUTES

SHOPPING LIST

- ¾ cup all-purpose flour
- 2 large eggs
- 1½ cups panko breadcrumbs
- ¼ cup Parmesan cheese, grated
- 1 tablespoon mustard powder
- Salt and ground black pepper, as required
- 4 (6-ounces) (¼-inch thick) skinless, boneless
- chicken cutlets
- 1 lemon, cut into slices

DIRECTIONS

1. In a shallow bowl, add the flour.
2. In a second bowl, crack the eggs and beat
3. well.
4. In a third bowl, mix the breadcrumbs, cheese, mustard powder, salt, and black pepper.
5. Season the chicken with salt, and black pepper.
6. Coat the chicken with flour, then dip into beaten eggs and finally coat with the breadcrumbs mixture.
7. Set the temperature of the Air Fryer to 355° F. Grease an Air Fryer basket. Arrange chicken cutlets into the prepared Air Fryer basket in a single layer.
8. Air Fry for about 30 minutes. Serve hot with the topping of lemon slices.

30 MINUTES

4

Breaded Chicken Tenderloins

BASIC RECIPE

NUTRITION

Calories 271
Carbs 12g
Protein 30.4g
Fat 11.5g
Sugar 0.9g
Sodium 113mg

DIRECTIONS

1. In a shallow dish, beat the egg.
2. In another dish, add the oil and breadcrumbs and mix until a crumbly mixture forms.
3. Dip the chicken tenderloins into beaten egg and then coat with the breadcrumbs mixture.
4. Shake off the excess coating.
5. Set the temperature of the Air Fryer to 35°F.
6. Grease an Air Fryer basket. Arrange chicken tenderloins into the prepared Air Fryer basket in a single layer.
7. Air Fry for about 12-15 minutes.
8. Remove from Air Fryer and transfer the chicken thighs onto a serving platter.
9. Serve hot.

15 MINUTES

15 MINUTES

4

SHOPPING LIST

- 1 egg, beaten
- 2 tablespoons vegetable oil
- ½ cup breadcrumbs
- 8 skinless, boneless chicken tenderloins

Herb Crusted Roast

INTERMEDIATE RECIPE

NUTRITION

Calories 457
Total Fat 22.64g
Total Carbs 2.84g
Fiber 0.7g
Protein 61.02g
Sugar 0.13g
Sodium 1056mg

SHOPPING LIST

- 2 tsp garlic powder
- 2 tsp onion powder
- 2 tsp dried basil
- 2 tsp dried parsley
- 2 tsp dried thyme
- ½ tbsp salt
- 1 tsp black pepper
- 2 lbs. beef roast
- 1 tbsp olive oil

25 MINUTES

DIRECTIONS

1. Insert the dripping pan at the bottom of the air fryer and preheat the oven at Roast mode at 390°F for 2 to 3 minutes.
2. In a small bowl, mix all the ingredients except for the meat and olive oil.
3. Rub the herb mixture all around the meat making sure to press the herb mix onto the meat to stick.
4. Allow marinating for 20 minutes at room temperature.
5. Grease the cooking tray with olive oil and set the roast on top. Slide the cooking pan onto the middle rack of the oven, and close the air fryer.
6. Set the timer for 15 minutes and press Start.
7. After 15 minutes, turn the roast over, close the oven, and reduce the temperature to 360°F.
8. Cook at a set time of 60 minutes in the same mode or until the meat is done.
9. Transfer the meat to a clean, flat surface when ready, allow sitting for 15 minutes, slice, and serve afterward.

90 MINUTES

4

Memphis Style Pork Ribs

INTERMEDIAT
RECIPE

DIRECTIONS

1. Insert the dripping pan onto the bottom part of the oven and preheat at Air Fry mode at 350^{0}F for 2 to 3 minutes.
2. In a small bowl, mix all the ingredients up to the spare ribs and rub the spice mixture on all sides of each rib.
3. Arrange the 4 to 6 ribs on the cooking tray, slide the tray onto the middle rack of the oven, and close the oven.
4. Set the timer for 35 minutes, and press Start.
5. Cook until the ribs are golden brown and tender within while flipping every halfway.
6. Transfer to a plate when ready and allow cooling for 2 to 3 minutes before serving.

10 MINUTES

38 MINUTES

4

SHOPPING LIST

- 1 tsp garlic powder
- 1 tsp onion powder
- 1 tbsp salt
- ½ tsp black pepper
- 1 tsp beef seasoning
- ½ tsp mustard powder
- 1 tbsp dark brown sugar
- 1 tbsp sweet paprika
- 2 ¼ lbs. pork spareribs, individually cut

NUTRITION

Calories 618
Total Fat 35.7g
Total Carbs 2.23g
Fiber 0.9g
Protein 67.75g
Sugar 0.24g
Sodium 1899mg

Thyme Roasted Pork Chops

ASIC RECIPE

DIRECTIONS

Insert the dripping pan onto the bottom part of the oven and preheat at Roast mode at 400°F for 2 to 3 minutes.

Brush the meat on both sides with olive oil and season with garlic powder, thyme, salt, and black pepper.

Place two chops on the cooking tray, slide the tray onto the middle rack of the oven and close.

4. Set the timer to 20 or 25 minutes depending on your desired doneness and press Start.
5. Cook until the timer ends or until the meat is golden brown and tender while flipping halfway.
6. Transfer to serving plates and cook the other two chops in the same manner.
7. Serve the chops immediately with buttered vegetables.

10 MINUTES | 25 MINUTES | 4

SHOPPING LIST

- 4 pork chops bone-in, loin, about 3/4-inch
- thickness
- 1 tbsp olive oil
- ¼ tsp garlic powder
- ¼ tsp dried thyme
- Salt and black pepper to taste

NUTRITION

alories 363 | Total Carbs 1.22g | Protein 40.47g | Sodium 87mg
otal Fat 20.76g | Fiber 0.2g | Sugar 0.58g

Yogurt Garlic Chicken

BASIC RECIPE

NUTRITION

Calories 380
Protein 26.0 g
Fat 15.0 g
Carbohydrates 34.0 g

DIRECTIONS

1. Mix the yogurt (1/2 cup), garlic cloves (4 pieces), olive oil (1 tablespoon), salt (1 teaspoon), lemon juice (2 tablespoons), pepper (1/4 teaspoon), allspice, cumin, and pepper flakes. Stir in the chicken and coat well.
2. Cover and marinate in the fridge for two hours.
3. Preheat the air fryer at 400°F
4. Grease a rimmed baking sheet (18x13-inch) with cooking spray.
5. Toss the bell peppers and onion with remaining olive oil (2 tablespoons), pepper (1/4 teaspoon), and salt (1/2 teaspoon).
6. Arrange veggies on the baking sheet's left side and the marinated chicken thighs (drain first) on the right side. Cook in the air fryer for twenty-five to thirty minutes.
7. Mix the yogurt sauce ingredients.
8. Slice air-fried chicken into half-inch strips. Top each pita round with chicken strips, roasted veggies, cucumbers, and yogurt sauce.

30 MINUTES

60 MINUTES

6

SHOPPING LIST

- Pita bread rounds, halved (6 pieces), English cucumber, sliced thinly, w/ each slice halved (1 cup)
- Olive oil (3 tablespoons)
- Black pepper, freshly ground (1/2 teaspoon)
- Chicken thighs, skinless, boneless (20 ounces)
- Bell pepper, red, sliced into half-inch portions (1 piece)
- Garlic cloves, chopped finely (4 pieces)
- Cumin, ground (1/2 teaspoon)
- Red onion, medium, sliced into half-inch, wedges (1 piece)
- Yogurt, plain, fat-free (1/2 cup), Lemon juice (2 tablespoons)
- Salt (1 ½ teaspoons), Red pepper flakes, crushed (1/2 teaspoon), Allspice, ground (1/2 teaspoon)
- Bell pepper, yellow, sliced into half-inch, portions (1 piece)
- Yogurt sauce, Olive oil (2 tablespoons), Salt (1/4 teaspoon)
- Parsley, flat-leaf, chopped finely (1 tablespoon)

Lemony Parmesan Salmon

INTERMEDIATE RECIPES

NUTRITION

Calories 290
Fat 16.0 g
Protein 33.0 g
Carbohydrates 4.0 g

10 MINUTES
25 MINUTES
4

DIRECTIONS

1. Preheat the air fryer at 350°F.
2. Mist cooking sprays onto a baking pan (shallow). Fill with pat-dried salmon. Brush salmon with butter (1 tablespoon) before sprinkling with salt.
3. Combine the breadcrumbs with onions, thyme, lemon peel, cheese, and remaining butter (1 tablespoon).
4. Cover salmon with the breadcrumb mixture.
5. Air-fry for fifteen to twenty-five minutes.

SHOPPING LIST

- Butter, melted (2 tablespoons)
- Green onions, sliced thinly (2 tablespoons)
- Breadcrumbs, white, fresh (3/4 cup)
- Thyme leaves, dried (1/4 teaspoon)
- Salmon fillet, 1 ¼-pound (1 piece)
- Salt (1/4 teaspoon)
- Parmesan cheese, grated (1/4 cup)
- Lemon peel, grated (2 teaspoons)
- cooking spray

Easiest Tuna Cobbler Ever

BASIC RECIPE

NUTRITION

Calories 320

Fat 11.0 g

Protein 28.0 g

Carbohydrates 31.0 g

SHOPPING LIST

- Water, cold (1/3 cup)
- Tuna, canned, drained (10 ounces)
- Sweet pickle relish (2 tablespoons)
- Mixed vegetables, frozen (1 ½ cups)
- Soup, cream of chicken, condensed (10 ¾
- ounces)
- Pimientos, sliced, drained (2 ounces)
- Lemon juice (1 teaspoon)
- Paprika

DIRECTIONS

1. Preheat the air fryer at 375°F.
2. Mist cooking spray into a round casserole (1
3. ½ quarts).
4. Mix the frozen vegetables with milk, soup, lemon juice, relish, pimientos, and tuna in a saucepan.
5. Cook for six to eight minutes over medium heat.
6. Fill the casserole with the tuna mixture.
7. Mix the biscuit mix with cold water to form a soft dough.
8. Beat for half a minute before dropping by four spoonfuls into the casserole.
9. Dust the dish with paprika before air-frying for twenty to twenty-five minutes.

Deliciously Homemade Pork Buns

BASIC RECIPE

NUTRITION

Calories 240
Fat 9.0 g
Protein 8.0 g
Carbohydrates 29.0 g

SHOPPING LIST

- Green onions, sliced thinly (3 pieces)
- Egg, beaten (1 piece)
- Pulled pork, diced, w/ barbecue sauce (1 cup)
- Buttermilk biscuits, refrigerated (16 1/3 ounces)
- Soy sauce (1 teaspoon)

DIRECTIONS

Preheat the air fryer at 325°F

Use parchment paper to line your baking sheet.

Combine pork with green onions.

Separate and press the dough to form 8 four-inch rounds.

Fill each biscuit round's center with two tablespoons of pork mixture. Cover with the dough edges and seal by pinching.

6. Arrange the buns on the sheet and brush with a mixture of soy sauce and egg.
7. Cook in the air fryer for twenty to twentyfive minutes.

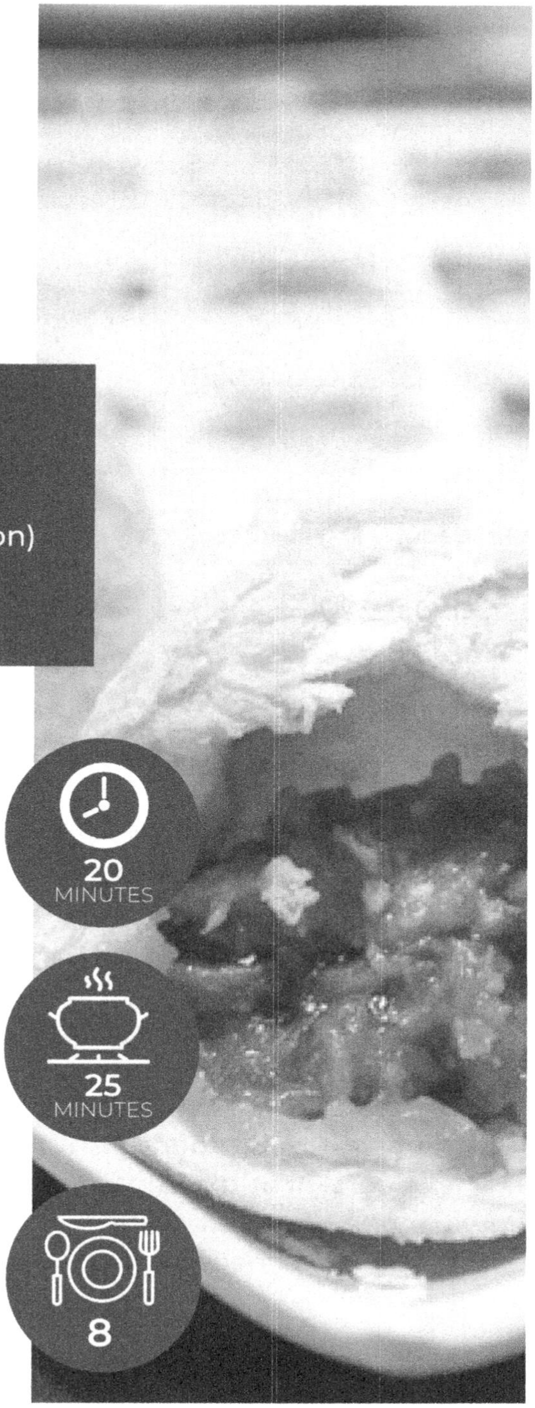

Mouthwatering Tuna Melts

BASIC RECIPE

SHOPPING LIST

- Salt (1/8 teaspoon)
- Onion, chopped (1/3 cup)
- Biscuits, refrigerated, flaky layers (16 1/3
- ounces)
- Tuna, water-packed, drained (10 ounces)
- Mayonnaise (1/3 cup)
- Pepper (1/8 teaspoon)
- Cheddar cheese, shredded (4 ounces)
- Tomato, chopped
- Sour cream
- Lettuce, shredded

NUTRITION

Calories 320
Fat 18.0 g
Protein 14.0 g
Carbohydrates 27.0 g

15 MINUTES

20 MINUTES

8

DIRECTIONS

1. Preheat the air fryer at 325°F
2. Mist cooking sprays onto a cookie sheet.
3. Mix tuna with mayonnaise, pepper, salt, and onion.
4. Separate dough so you have 8 biscuits; press each into 5-inch rounds.
5. Arrange 4 biscuit rounds on the sheet. Fill at the center with tuna mixture before topping with cheese.
6. Cover with the remaining biscuit rounds and press to seal.
7. Air-fry for fifteen to twenty minutes.
8. Slice each sandwich into halves.
9. Serve each piece topped with lettuce, tomato, and sour cream.

Bacon Wings

BASIC RECIPE

SHOPPING LIST

- Bacon strips (12 pieces)
- Paprika (1 teaspoon)
- Black pepper (1 tablespoon)
- Oregano (1 teaspoon)
- Chicken wings (12 pieces)
- Kosher salt (1 tablespoon)
- Brown sugar (1 tablespoon)
- Chili powder (1 teaspoon)
- Celery sticks
- Blue cheese dressing

DIRECTIONS

1. Preheat the air fryer at 325°F
2. Mix sugar, salt, chili powder, oregano, pepper, and paprika.
3. Coat chicken wings with this dry rub.
4. Wrap a bacon strip around each wing.
5. Arrange wrapped wings in the air fryer basket.
6. Cook for thirty minutes on each side in the air fryer. Let cool for five minutes.
7. Serve and enjoy with celery and blue cheese.

15 MINUTES

75 MINUTES

12

NUTRITION

Calories 100
Fat 5.0 g
Protein 10.0 g
Carbohydrates 2.0 g

Pepper Pesto Lamb

INTERMEDIATE RECIPE

NUTRITION

Calories 310
Protein 40.0 g
Fat 15.0 g
Carbohydrates 1.0 g

DIRECTIONS

1. Preheat the oven at 325°F.
2. Mix the pesto ingredients in the food processor.
3. Unroll the lamb and cover the cut side with pesto.
4. Top with roasted peppers before rolling up the lamb and tying with kitchen twine.
5. Coat lamb with seasoning (lemon pepper) and air-fry for one hour.

SHOPPING LIST

- Pesto ingredients:
- Rosemary leaves, fresh (1/4 cup)
- Garlic cloves (3 pieces)
- Parsley, fresh, packed firmly (3/4 cup)
- Mint leaves, fresh (1/4 cup)
- Olive oil (2 tablespoons)
- Lamb ingredients:
- Red bell peppers, roasted, drained (7 ½ ounces)
- Leg of lamb, boneless, rolled (5 pounds)
- Seasoning, lemon pepper (2 teaspoons)

15 MINUTES

75 MINUTES

12

Tuna Spinach Casserole

BASIC RECIPE

NUTRITION

Calories 400
Protein 21.0 g
Fat 19.0 g
Carbohydrates 35.0 g

DIRECTIONS

1. Preheat the oven to 350^{0}F.
2. Mist cooking sprays onto a glass baking dish (11x7-inch).
3. Follow package directions in cooking and draining the noodles.
4. Stir the cheese (1 ½ cups) and soup together in a skillet heated on medium.
5. Once cheese melts, stir in your noodles, milk, spinach, tuna, and lemon peel.
6. Once bubbling, pour into the prepped dish.
7. Unroll the dough and sprinkle with remaining cheese (1/2 cup).
8. Roll up dough and pinch at the seams to seal. Slice into 8 portions and place over the tuna mixture.
9. Air-fry for twenty to twenty-five minutes

SHOPPING LIST

- Mushroom soup, creamy (18 ounces)
- Milk (1/2 cup)
- White tuna, solid, in-water, drained (12
- ounces)
- Crescent dinner rolls, refrigerated (8 ounces)
- Egg noodles, wide, uncooked (8 ounces)
- Cheddar cheese, shredded (2 cups)
- Spinach, chopped, frozen, thawed, drained (9 ounces)
- Lemon peel grated (2 teaspoons)
- Cooking spray

Crispy Hot Sauce Chicken

BASIC RECIPE

NUTRITION

Calories 695
Total Fat 17.5 g
Saturated Fat 4.8 g
Cholesterol 283 mg
Sodium 355 mg
Total Carbs 6.4 g
Fiber 1.8 g
Sugar 0.8 g
Protein 117.4 g

DIRECTIONS

1. Whisk hot sauce with buttermilk in a large bowl.
2. Add chicken pieces to the buttermilk mixture and marinate for 1 hour in the refrigerator.
3. Dredge the chicken through seasoned flour and shake off the excess.
4. Place the coated chicken in the air fryer basket and spray them with cooking oil.
5. Return the fryer basket to the air fryer and cook on air fry mode for 30 minutes at 380°F.
6. Flip the chicken pieces once cooked half way through.
7. Enjoy right away.

5 MINUTES

30 MINUTES

4

SHOPPING LIST

- 2 cups buttermilk
- 1 tablespoon hot sauce
- 1 whole chicken, cut up
- 1 cup kentucky kernel flour
- Oil for spraying

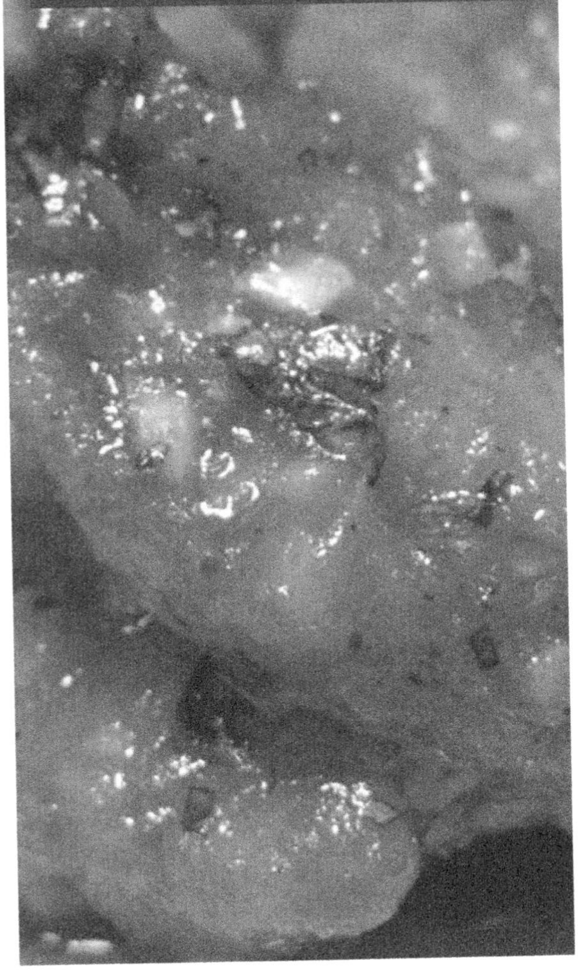

Teriyaki Chicken Meatballs

INTERMEDIATE RECIPE

NUTRITION

Calories 401
Total Fat 8.9 g
Saturated Fat 4.5 g
Cholesterol 57 mg
Sodium 340 mg
Total Carbs 24.7 g
Fiber 1.2 g
Sugar 1.3 g
Protein 55.3 g

5 MINUTES

SHOPPING LIST

- For Chicken Meatballs
- 1 lb. ground chicken
- ½ cup gluten-free oat flour
- 1 small onion, chopped
- ¾ teaspoon garlic powder
- ¾ teaspoon crushed chili flakes
- 1 teaspoon dried cilantro leaves
- Salt, to taste
- Scallions, for garnish
- Sesame seeds, for garnish
- For Spicy Teriyaki Sauce
- ¼ cup sweet and sour sauce
- 2 tbsps.ricevinegar
- 2 tbsps.soy sauce (light)
- 2 tbsps.honey
- ½ teaspoon hot sauce (optional)
- 1 teaspoon crushed chili flakes
- ¾ top garlic powder
- ¾ teaspoon ginger powde

DIRECTIONS

1. Add the ingredients for the meatballs to a suitable bowl.
2. Mix well and knead the dough.
3. Make small meatballs out of this dough and place them in the air fryer basket.
4. Spray them with cooking oil.
5. Return the fryer basket to the air fryer and cook on air fry mode for 10 minutes at 350°F.
6. Meanwhile, mix all the ingredients for the teriyaki sauce in a saucepan.
7. Stir and cook this sauce until it thickens, Add the air-fried balls to the sauce.
8. Garnish with scallions and sesame seeds.
9. Enjoy.

10 MINUTES

4

Orange Tofu

BASIC RECIPE

DIRECTIONS

Dice the squeezed tofu into cubes then place them in a Ziploc bag.
Add tamari and 1 tablespoon of cornstarch to the tofu.
Seal the tofu bag and shake well to coat.
Spread this tofu in the air fryer basket and spray them with cooking oil.
Return the fryer basket to the air fryer and cook on air fry mode for 15 minutes at 350° F.
7. Air fry the tofu cubes in two batches.
8. Mix all the ingredients for the sauce in a saucepan and stir cook until it thickens.
9. Toss in fried tofu and mix well.
10. Enjoy.

SHOPPING LIST

- 1 lb. extra-firm tofu, drained and pressed
- 1 tablespoon tamari
- 1 tablespoon cornstarch
- For Sauce:
- 1 teaspoon orange zest
- 1/3 cup orange juice
- ½ cup water
- 2 teaspooncornstarch
- ¼ teaspoon crushed red pepper flakes
- 1 teaspoon fresh ginger, minced
- 1 teaspoon fresh garlic, minced
- 1 table spoon pure maple syrup

NUTRITION

alories 427 Total
t 31.1 g
turated Fat 4.2 g
Cholesterol 123 mg
Sodium 86 mg
Total Carbs 9 g
Sugar 12.4 g
Fiber 19.8 g
Protein 23.5 g

Madagascan Stew

BASIC RECIPE

5 MINUTES

19 MINUTES

4

DIRECTIONS

1. Cut the potatoes into quarters and toss them with cooking oil.
2. Place the potatoes in the air fryer basket.
3. Add onion to the basket and continue air frying for another 4 minutes.
4. Transfer them to a saucepan and place over medium heat. Add garlic, ginger, beans, tomatoes, seasoning, vegetable stock, and tomato puree.
5. Mix cornstarch with water in a bowl and pour into the pan.
6. Simmer this mixture for 15 minutes.
7. Add arugula and cook for another 4 minutes.
8. Serve with rice.

SHOPPING LIST

- 7 oz. baby new potatoes
- 1 tablespoon oil
- ½ onion, finely diced
- 1 ¼ cups canned black beans, drained
- 1 ¼ cups canned kidney beans, drained
- 3 cloves garlic, minced
- 1 tablespoon pureed ginger
- 2 large tomatoes, chopped
- 1 tablespoon tomato puree
- Salt, Black pepper
- 1 cup vegetable stock
- ½ tablespoon cornstarch
- 1 tablespoon water
- 1 large handful of arugula
- Cooked rice, to serve (optional)

NUTRITION

Calories 398	Cholesterol 200 mg	Fiber 1 g
Total Fat 13.8 g	Sodium 272 mg	Sugar 1.3 g
Saturated Fat 5.1 g	Total Carbs 53.6 g	Protein 11.8 g

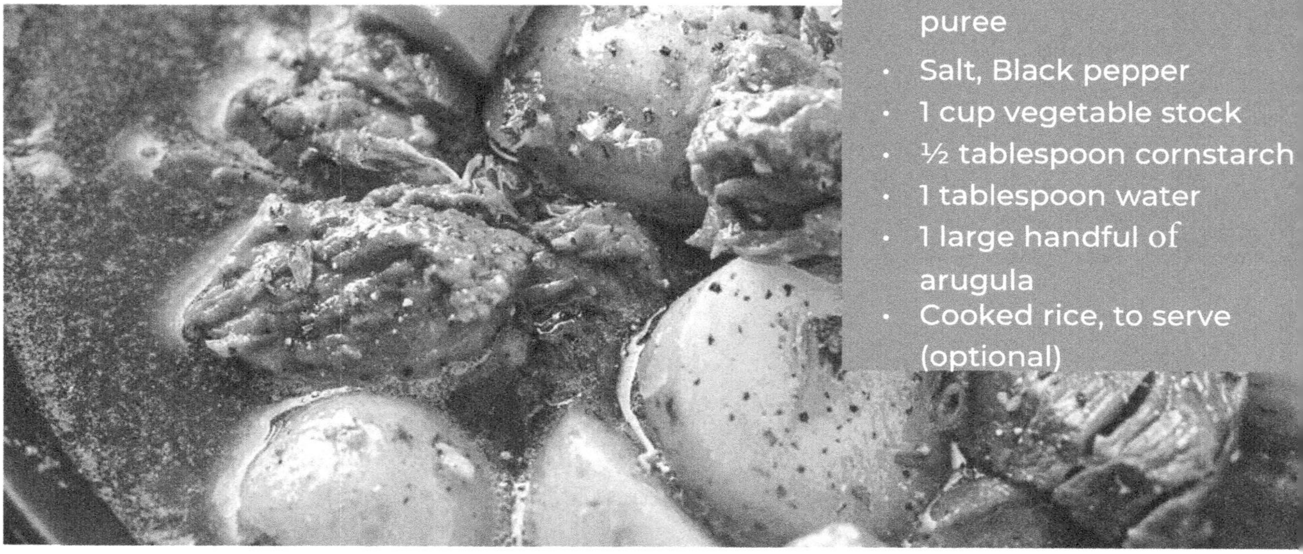

Bacon Cheddar Chicken Fingers

BASIC RECIPE

NUTRITION

Calories 341 Fat 11g
Saturated Fat 4g
Trans Fat 0g
Cholesterol 31.5g
Fiber 1g
Sodium 297mg
Protein 28g

DIRECTIONS

1. Set the air fryer to the temperature of 360°F. In a glass dish, whip the water and eggs until just combined.
2. Use a zip-top bag, shake the garlic powder, salt, breadcrumbs, cayenne, onion powder, and pepper together.
3. Immerse the chicken into the eggs and shake in the Ziploc bag until fully covered.
4. Dip again in the egg mixture and back into the seasonings until a thick coating is present.
5. Remove the tenders from the bag and set them in the frying pan in the basket. Do them in batches if need to not over-pack the pan.
6. Apply the canola oil spray to the top of the tenders and heat for 6 minutes.
7. Flip the tenders to the other side. Steam for another 4 minutes.
8. Blend the bacon bits and shredded cheese in a dish.
9. Evenly dust the bacon and cheese onto the hot tenders and fry for 2 more minutes.
10. Remove and serve while hot.

SHOPPING LIST

- For the chicken fingers:
- 1 lb. chicken tenders, about 8 pieces
- Cooking spray (canola oil)
- Cheddar cheese - 1 cup, shredded
- Two eggs, large
- 1/3 cup bacon bits
- 2 tablespoon water
- For the breading:
- 1 teaspoon of onion powder
- Panko breadcrumbs - 2 cups
- Black pepper - 1 teaspoon, freshly ground
- Paprika - 2 tablespoon
- Garlic powder - 1 teaspoon
- Salt - 2 teaspoon

10 MINUTES

20 MINUTES

4

Battered Cod

INTERMEDIATE RECIPES

10 MINUTES

30 MINUTES

4

NUTRITION

Calories 245
Fat 11g
Cholesterol 31.5g
Fiber 1g
Sodium 297mg
Protein 28g

DIRECTIONS

1. Whip the eggs in a glass dish until smooth and set to the side. In a separate dish, blend the cornstarch, salt, almond flour, garlic powder, parsley, and onion powder, whisking to remove any lumpiness.
2. Immerse the pieces of cods into the egg and then into the spiced flour, covering completely.
3. Transfer to the fryer basket in a single layer. Heat the fish for 7 minutes at a temperature of 350°F. Turn the cod over and steam for an additional 7 minutes.

SHOPPING LIST

- 20 oz. cod
- 1/4 teaspoon salt
- 8 oz. all-purpose flour
- 1 tablespoon parsley seasoning
- 3 teaspoon cornstarch
- 1/2 teaspoon garlic powder
- Two eggs, preferably large
- 1/2 teaspoon onion powder

Beef Kabobs

BASIC RECIPE

NUTRITION

Calories 261
Fat 11g
Cholesterol 31.5g
Fiber 1g
Sodium 297mg
Protein 28g

SHOPPING LIST

- 1/3 cup low-fat sour cream
- One bell pepper
- 16 oz. Of beef chuck ribs, boneless
- 2 tablespoon soy sauce
- 8 6-inch skewers
- 1/4 teaspoon pepper
- 1/2 medium onion

DIRECTIONS

1. Slice the ribs into pieces about 1-inch wide
2. In a lidded tub, combine the soy sauce, ribs and sour cream making sure the meat is fully covered.
3. Refrigerate for half an hour at least, if not overnight.
4. Immerse the wooden skewers for approximately 10 minutes in water.
5. Set the temperature of the air fryer to 400°F.
6. Slice the onion and bell pepper into 1-inch pieces.
7. Remove the meat from the marinade, draining well.
8. Layer the onions, beef and bell peppers on the skewers and dust with pepper.
9. Heat for 10 minutes, ensuring you spin the skewers 5 minutes into cooking time.
10. Serve while hot and enjoy.

Cheese Dogs

BASIC RECIPE

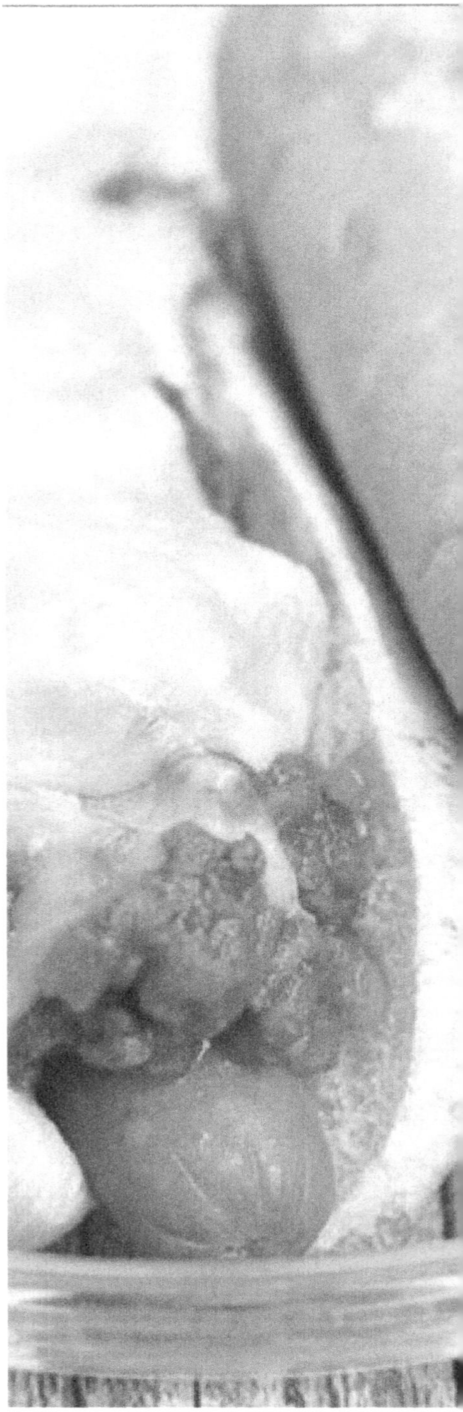

NUTRITION

Calories 432
Fat 11g
Cholesterol 31.5g
Fiber 1g
Sodium 297mg
Protein 28g

SHOPPING LIST

- 4 hotdogs
- 1/4 cup your choice of cheese, grated
- 4 hotdog buns

DIRECTIONS

1. Adjust the air fryer to heat at a the temperature of 390°F for approximately 5 minutes.
2. Set the hot dogs in the basket and broil for 5 minutes.
3. Remove and create the hot dog with the bun and cheese as desired and move back to the basket for another 2 minutes.
4. Remove and enjoy while hot.

10 MINUTES

15 MINUTES

4

Chicken Cordon Bleu

BASIC RECIPE

SHOPPING LIST

- 1/4 teaspoon pepper
- 4 chicken paillards
- 1/4 teaspoon salt
- 8 slices swiss cheese
- 1/2 cup all-purpose flour
- 2/3 cup parmesan cheese, grated
- 1 1/2 cup panko breadcrumbs
- 8 slices ham
- Two eggs, large
- 2 tablespoon dijon mustard
- 8 toothpicks
- Grape seed oil spray

DIRECTIONS

1. On a piece of baking lining, brush the Dijon mustard on each chicken paillard and sprinkle with pepper and salt Layer 1 cheese, 2 slices of the ham and then the additional slice of cheese on each of the pieces of chicken.
2. Rotate the chicken beginning with the longer side to create a roll.
3. Fasten in place with two toothpicks.
4. Whip the egg in one dish, empty the flour into a second dish and blend the parmesan cheese and breadcrumbs into a third.
5. Immerse one chicken first in flour, secondly immerse in the egg and then roll the chicken completely in the breadcrumbs.
6. Press the cheese and breadcrumbs into the chicken to secure and place onto a plate.
7. Repeat for the other pieces of chicken. Apply the grape seed oil spray to each piece of chicken and transfer to the air fryer basket after 5 minutes.
8. Set the air fryer temperature to heat at 350°F.
9. Grill for 8 minutes and carefully turn the chicken to the other side. Heat for an additional 8 minutes.
10. Remove to a serving dish and wait approximately 5 minutes before serving hot.

NUTRITION

Calories 548
Fat 11g
Cholesterol 31.5g
Fiber 1g
Sodium 297mg
Protein 28g

10 MINUTES

35 MINUTES

4

Cheeseburger Patties

BASIC RECIPE

SHOPPING LIST

- 1/2 clove garlic, minced
- 1 1/3 cup ground beef
- 4 oz onion, diced
- 2 tablespoon worcestershire sauce
- one egg, large
- 2 oz. panko breadcrumbs
- 1/8 teaspoon cayenne pepper
- cooking spray (olive oil)
- 1/4 teaspoon salt
- 4 slices of cheese of your choice
- 1/8 teaspoon pepper

NUTRITION

Calories 367
Fat 11g
Saturated Fat 4g
Trans Fat 0g
Cholesterol 31.5g
Fiber 1g
Sodium 297mg
Protein 28g

10 MINUTES

20 MINUTES

4

DIRECTIONS

1. Using a big glass dish, combine the diced onion, pepper, minced garlic, cayenne pepper, breadcrumbs, and salt until incorporated.
2. Blend the ground beef, Worcestershire sauce, and egg and integrate thoroughly by hand.
3. Form the meat into 4 individual patties and move to the air fryer basket.
4. Coat the patties with cooking spray.
5. Adjust the temperature for 375°F and heat for 8 minutes.
6. Turn the burgers over and steam for an additional 2 minutes.
7. Cover with a slice of cheese and continue cooking for approximately 3 minutes.
8. Enjoy as-is or place on a bun with your favorite toppings.

Country Meatballs

BASIC RECIPE

NUTRITION

Calories 432
Fat 11g
Saturated Fat 4g
Trans Fat 0g
Cholesterol 31.5g
Fiber 1g
Sodium 297mg
Protein 28g

DIRECTIONS

1. Whisk the oregano, breadcrumbs, chopped garlic, and salt, chopped parsley, pepper, and grated Parmigiano-Reggiano cheese until combined.
2. Blend the ground beef and egg into the mixture using your hands.
3. Incorporate the ingredients thoroughly.
4. Divide the meat into 12 pieces and roll into rounds.
5. Coat the inside of the basket with avocado oil spray to grease. Adjust the temperature to 350°F and heat for approximately 12 minutes.
6. Roll the meatballs over and steam for another 4 minutes and remove to a serving plate.
7. Enjoy as-is or combine with your favorite pasta or sauce.

SHOPPING LIST

- One egg, large
- 16 oz. Ground beef
- 1/8 teaspoon pepper
- 1/2 teaspoon oregano seasoning
- 1 1/4 cup breadcrumbs
- 1/2 clove garlic, chopped
- 1 oz parsley, chopped
- 1/4 teaspoon salt -
- 1 oz. Cup Parmigiano-reggiano cheese,
- grated
- Cooking spray (avocado oil)

10 MINUTES

35 MINUTES

3

Loaded Baked Potatoes

BASIC RECIPE

NUTRITION

alories 253
at 32g
aturated Fat 10g
rans Fat 0g
Cholesterol 31.5g
Fiber 1g
Sodium 297mg
Protein 28g

25 MINUTES

4

10 MINUTES

SHOPPING LIST

- 1/3 cup milk
- 2 oz. sour cream
- 1/3 cup white cheddar, grated
- 2 oz. Parmesan cheese, grated
- 1/8 teaspoon garlic salt
- 6 oz. ham, diced
- 2 medium russet potatoes
- 4 oz. sharp cheddar, shredded
- 1/8 cup. Green onion, diced

DIRECTIONS

Puncture the potatoes deeply with a fork a few times and microwave for approximately 5 minutes.

Flip them to the other side and nuke for an additional 5 minutes. The potatoes should be soft.

Use oven mitts to remove from the microwave and cut them in halves.

Spoon out the insides of the potatoes to about a quarter-inch from the skins and distribute the potato flesh to a glass bowl.

Combine the parmesan, garlic salt, sour cream, and white cheddar cheese to the potato dish and incorporate fully.

7. Distribute the mixture back to the emptied potato skins. Create a small hollow in the middle by pressing with a spoon.
8. Divide the ham evenly between the potatoes and place the ham inside the hollow.
9. Position the potatoes in the fryer and set the air fryer to the temperature of 300°F.
10. Heat for 8 minutes and then sprinkle the cheddar cheese on top of each potato.
11. Melt the cheese for two more minutes than serve with diced onions on top.

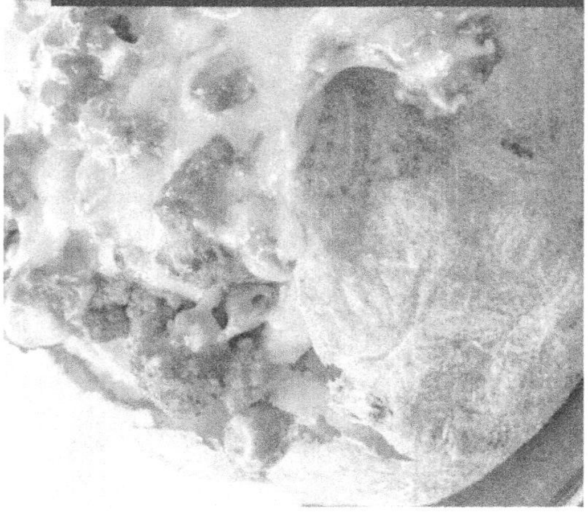

Pepperoni Pizza

BASIC RECIPE

NUTRITION

Calories 270
Fat 11g
Saturated Fat 4g
Trans Fat 0g
Cholesterol 31.5g
Fiber 1g
Sodium 297mg
Protein 28g

DIRECTIONS

1. Prepare the naan flatbread by brushed the olive oil on the top.
2. Layer the naan with pizza sauce, mozzarella cheese, and pepperoni.
3. Transfer to the frying basket and set the air fryer to the temperature of 375°F.
4. Heat for approximately 6 minutes and enjoy immediately.

SHOPPING LIST

- 1 mini naan flatbread
- 2 tablespoon pizza sauce
- 7 slices mini pepperoni
- 1 tablespoon olive oil
- 2 tablespoon mozzarella cheese, shredded

10 MINUTES

10 MINUTES

1

Southern Style Fried Chicken

BASIC RECIPE

NUTRITION

Calories 390
Fat 11g
Saturated Fat 4g
Trans Fat 0g
Cholesterol 31.5g
Fiber 1g
Sodium 297mg
Protein 28g

10 MINUTES

25 MINUTES

6

SHOPPING LIST

- 1 teaspoon italian seasoning
- 2 lbs. chicken legs or breasts
- 2 tablespoon buttermilk
- 1 1/2teaspoon paprika seasoning
- 2 oz. cornstarch
- 1 teaspoon onion powder
- 3 teaspoons hot sauce
- 1 1/2 teaspoon pepper
- 2 large eggs
- 1 cup self-rising flour
- 2 teaspoon salt
- Cooking spray (olive oil)
- 1/4 cup water
- 1 1/2teaspoon garlic powder

DIRECTIONS

1. Clean the chicken by washing thoroughly and pat dry with paper towels.
2. Use a glass dish to blend the pepper, paprika, garlic powder, onion powder, salt, and Italian seasoning.
3. Rub approximately 1 tablespoon of the spices into the pieces of chicken to cover entirely. Blend the cornstarch, flour, and spices by shaking in a large Ziploc bag.
4. In a separate dish, combine the eggs, hot sauce, water, and milk until integrated.
5. Completely cover the spiced chicken in the flour and then immerse in the eggs.
6. Coat in the flour for a second time and set on a tray for approximately 15 minutes. Before transferring the chicken to the air fryer, spray liberally with olive oil and space the pieces out, frying a separate batch if required.
7. Adjust the temperature to 350°F for approximately 18 minutes. Take the chicken out and set it on a plate. Wait about 5 minutes before serving.

Stuffed Bell Peppers

BASIC RECIPE

NUTRITION

Calories 341
Fat 11g
Saturated Fat 4g
Trans Fat 0g
Cholesterol 31.5g
Fiber 1g
Sodium 297mg
Protein 28g

SHOPPING LIST

- 1/2medium onion, chopped
- 4 oz. cheddar cheese, shredded
- 1/2 teaspoon pepper
- 8 oz. ground beef
- 1 teaspoon olive oil
- 4 oz. tomato sauce
- 1 teaspoon worcestershire sauce
- 2 medium green peppers, stems and seeds
- discarded
- 1 teaspoon salt, separated
- 4 cups of water
- 1 clove garlic, minced

10 MINUTES

30 MINUTES

2

DIRECTIONS

1. Boil the water in pot steam the green peppers with the tops and seeds removed with 1/2 teaspoon of the salt.
2. Move from the burner after approximately 3 minutes and drain.
3. Pat the peppers with paper towels to properly dry.
4. In a hot frying pan, melt the olive oil and toss the garlic and onion for approximately 2 minutes until browned. Drain thoroughly.
5. Set the air fryer temperature to 400°F to warm-up.
6. Using a glass dish, blend the beef along with Worcestershire sauce, 2 ounces of tomato sauce, salt, vegetables, 2 ounces of cheddar cheese and pepper until fully incorporated.
7. Spoon the mixture evenly into the peppers and drizzle the remaining 2 ounces of tomato sauce on top.
8. Then dust with the remaining 2 ounces of cheddar cheese.
9. Assemble the peppers in the basket of the air fryer and heat fully for approximately 18 minutes.
10. The meat should be fully cooked before removing.
11. Place on a platter and serve immediately.

Tuna Patties

BASIC RECIPE

DIRECTIONS

1. Set the temperature of the air fryer to 400°F.
2. Combine the almond flour, mayonnaise, salt, onion powder, dill, garlic powder and pepper using a food blender for approximately 30 seconds until incorporated.
3. Empty the canned tuna and lemon juice into the blender and pulse for an additional 30 seconds until integrated fully.
4. Divide evenly into 4 pieces and create patties by hand.
5. Transfer to the fryer basket in a single layer and heat for approximately 12 minutes.

10 MINUTES

20 MINUTES

4

SHOPPING LIST

- 1 teaspoon garlic powder
- 2 cans of tuna, in water
- 1 teaspoon dill seasoning
- 4 teaspoon all-purpose flour
- 1/4 teaspoon salt
- 4 teaspoon mayonnaise
- 2 tablespoon lemon juice
- 1/2 teaspoon onion powder
- 1/4 teaspoon pepper

NUTRITION

Calories 370	Fiber 1g
Fat 11g	Sodium 297mg
Cholesterol 31.5g	Protein 28g

Pork Chops

BASIC RECIPE

NUTRITION

Calories 441
Cal Carbs 28.6g
Fat 22.3g
Protein 30.6g
Fiber 0.5g

5 MINUTES

15 MINUTES

5

DIRECTIONS

1. Switch on the air fryer, insert fryer basket, grease it with olive oil, then shut with its lid, set the fryer at 350°F and preheat for 5 minutes.
2. Meanwhile, place bread slices in a food processor and pulse until the mixture resembles crumbs.
3. Tip the breadcrumbs in a shallow dish, add parsley, ½ teaspoon salt, ¼ teaspoon ground black pepper and stir until mixed.
4. Place flour in another shallow dish, add remaining salt and black pepper, along with pork seasoning and stir until mixed.
5. Crack the egg in a bowl, pour in apple juice and whisk until combined. Working on one pork chop at a time, first coat it into the flour mixture, then dip into egg and then evenly coat with breadcrumbs mixture.
6. Open the fryer, add coated pork chops in it in a single layer, close with its lid and cook for 10 minutes until nicely golden and cooked, flipping the pork chops halfway through the frying. When the air fryer beeps, open its lid, transfer pork chops onto a serving plate and serve.

SHOPPING LIST

- 4 slices of almond bread
- 5 pork chops, bone-in, pastured
- 3.5 ounces coconut flour
- 1 teaspoon salt
- 3 tablespoons parsley
- ½ teaspoon ground black pepper
- 1 tablespoon pork seasoning
- 2 tablespoons olive oil
- 1/3 cup apple juice, unsweetened
- 1 egg, pastured

Steak

BASIC RECIPES

10 MINUTES | 18 MINUTES | 2

NUTRITION

Calories 82
Cal Carbs 0g
Fat 5g
Protein 8.7g
Fiber 0g

DIRECTIONS

1. Switch on the air fryer, insert fryer basket, grease it with olive oil, then shut with its lid, set the fryer at 400 degrees F and preheat for 5 minutes.
2. Meanwhile, coat the steaks with oil and then season with black pepper, garlic, and salt.
3. Open the fryer, add steaks in it, close with its lid and cook 10 to 18 minutes until nicely golden and steaks are cooked to desired denseness, flipping the steaks halfway through the frying.
4. When the air fryer beeps, open its lid and transfer steaks to a cutting board.
5. Take two large pieces of aluminum foil, place a steak on each piece, top steak with ½ tablespoon butter, then cover with foil and let it rest for 5 minutes.
6. Serve straight away.

SHOPPING LIST

- 2 steaks, grass-fed, each about 6 ounces and
- ¾ inch thick
- 1 tablespoon butter, unsalted
- ¾ teaspoon ground black pepper
- 1/2 teaspoon garlic powder
- ¾ teaspoon salt
- 1 teaspoon olive oil

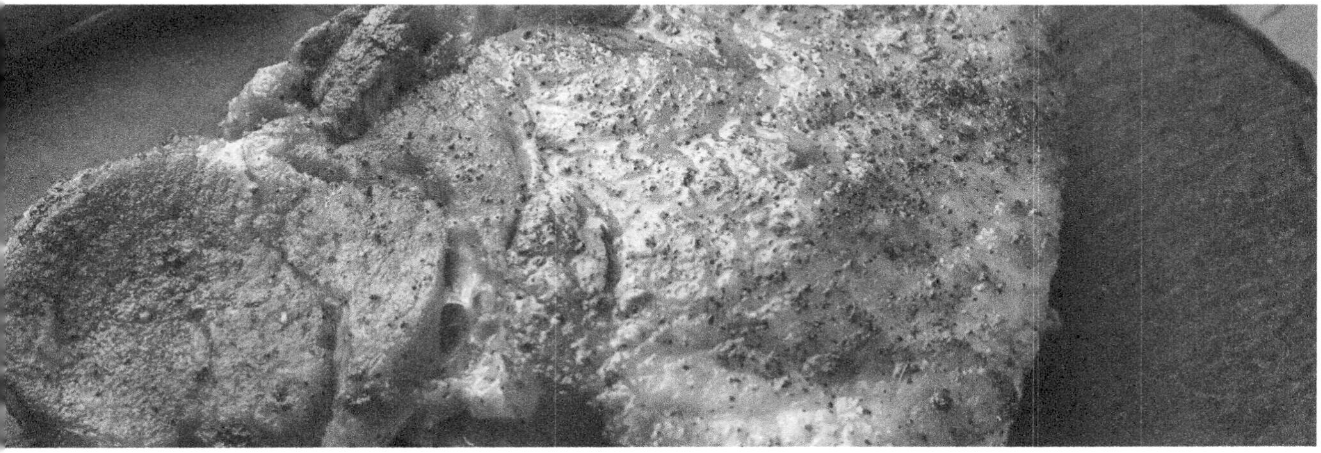

Quinoa and Spinach Cakes

BASIC RECIPE

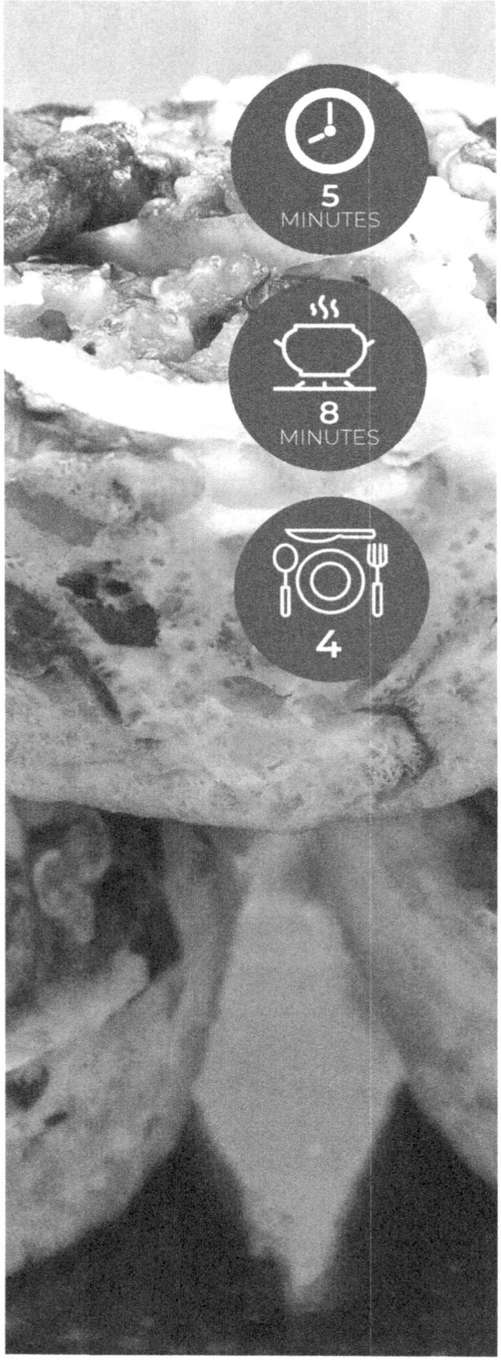

NUTRITION

Calories 188
Carbs 31.2g
Fat 4.4 g
Protein 8.1g

SHOPPING LIST

- 2 c. cooked quinoa
- 1 c. chopped baby spinach
- 1 egg
- 2 tbsps. Minced parsley
- 1 teaspoon minced garlic
- 1 carrot, peeled and shredded
- 1 chopped onion
- ¼ c. oat milk
- ¼ c. parmesan cheese, grated
- 1 c. breadcrumbs
- Sea salt
- Ground black

DIRECTIONS

1. In a mixing bowl, mix all ingredients.
2. Season with salt and pepper to taste.
3. Preheat your Air Fryer to 390°F.
4. Scoop ¼ cup of quinoa and spinach mixture and place in the Air Fryer cooking basket.
5. Cook in batches until browned for about 8 minutes.
6. Serve and enjoy!

Spinach in Cheese Envelopes

INTERMEDIATE RECIPE

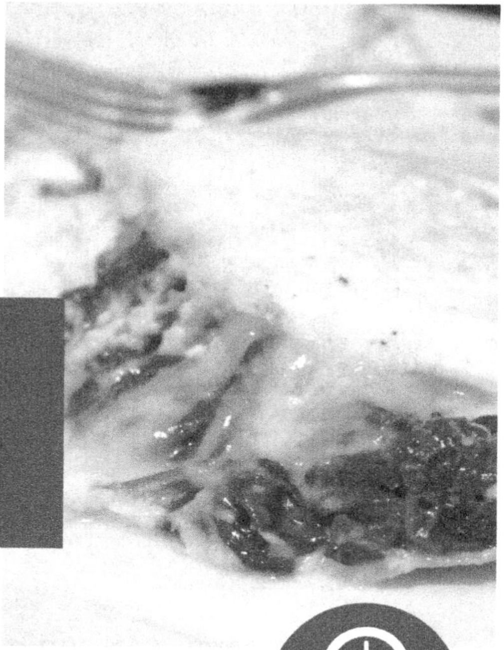

NUTRITION

Calories 365 | Protein 10.4g
Fat 34.6g | Carbs 4.4g

SHOPPING LIST

- 1½ c. almond flour
- 3 egg yolks
- 2 eggs
- ½ c. cheddar cheese
- 2 c. steamed spinach
- ¼ teaspoon salt
- ½ teaspoon pepper
- 3 c. cream cheese
- ¼ c. chopped onion

DIRECTIONS

Place cream cheese in a mixing bowl then whisks until soft and fluffy.

Add egg yolks to the mixing bowl then continue whisking until incorporated.

Stir in coconut flour into the cheese mixture then mix until becoming a soft dough.

Place the dough on a flat surface then roll until thin.

Cut the thin dough into 8 squares then keep.

Crash the eggs then place them in a bowl.

. Season with salt, pepper, and grated cheese, then mix well.

. Add chopped spinach and onion to the egg mixture, then stir until combined.

9. Put spinach filling on a square dough then fold until becoming an envelope. Repeat with the remaining spinach filling and dough.
10. Glue with water.
11. Preheat an Air Fryer to 425°F (218°C). Arrange the spinach envelopes in the Air Fryer then cook for 12 minutes or until lightly golden brown.
12. Remove from the Air Fryer then serve warm.
13. Enjoy!

5 MINUTES

12 MINUTES

8

Avocado Sticks

BASIC RECIPE

5 MINUTES

8 MINUTES

6

SHOPPING LIST

- 2 avocados
- 1 c. coconut flour
- 2 teaspoon Black pepper
- 3 egg yolks
- 1½ tbsps. Water
- ¼ teaspoon salt
- 1 c.vegan butter
- 2 teaspoon Minced garlic
- ¼ c. chopped parsley
- 1 tablespoon lemon juice

NUTRITION

Calories 340

Fat 33.8g

Protein 4.5g

Carbs 8.5g

DIRECTIONS

1. Place butter in a mixing bowl then adds minced garlic, chopped parsley, and lemon juice to the bowl.
2. Using an electric mixer mix until smooth and fluffy.
3. Transfer the garlic butter to a container with a lid then store in the fridge.
4. Peel the avocados then cut into wedges.
5. Set aside.
6. Put the egg yolks in a mixing bowl then pour water into it.
7. Season with salt and black pepper, then stir until incorporated.
8. Take an avocado wedge then roll in the coconut flour.
9. Dip in the egg mixture then returns to the coconut flour.
10. Roll until the avocado wedge is completely coated. Repeat with the remaining avocado wedges.
11. Preheat an Air Fryer to 400°F (204°C).
12. Arrange the coated avocado wedges in the Air Fryer basket then cook for 8 minutes or until golden.
13. Remove from the Air Fryer then arrange on a serving dish.
14. Serve with garlic butter then enjoy right away.

Chili Roasted Eggplant Soba

BASIC RECIPE

SHOPPING LIST

- 200g eggplants
- Kosher salt
- Ground black pepper
- Noodles:
- 8 oz. soba noodles
- 1 c. sliced button mushrooms
- 2 tbsps. Peanut oil
- 2 tbsps. Light soy sauce
- 1 Tablespoon rice vinegar
- 2 tbsps. Chopped cilantro
- 2 chopped red chili pepper
- 1 teaspoon sesame oil

DIRECTIONS

1. Wash eggplants and then slice into ¼-inch thick cuts.
2. Season with salt and pepper, to taste.
3. Preheat your Air Fryer to 390°F.
4. Place eggplants in the Air Fryer cooking basket. Cook for 10 minutes.
5. Meanwhile, cook the soba noodles according to packaging directions.
7. Drain the noodles. In a large mixing bowl, combine the peanut oil, soy sauce, rice vinegar, cilantro, chili, and sesame oil. Mix well.
8. Add the cooked soba noodles, mushrooms, and roasted eggplants; toss to coat.
9. Transfer mixture into the Air Fryer cooking basket. Cook for another 5 minutes.
10. Serve and enjoy!

10 MINUTES

15 MINUTES

4

NUTRITION

Calories 318
Fat 8.2g
Carbs 54g
Protein 11.3g.

Broccoli Popcorn

BASIC RECIPE

NUTRITION

Calories 202
Protein 5.1g
Fat 17.5g
Carbs 7.8g

SHOPPING LIST

- 2 c. broccoli florets
- 2 c. almond flour
- 4 egg yolks
- ½ teaspoon salt
- ½ teaspoon pepper

DIRECTIONS

1. Soak the broccoli florets in salty water to remove all the insects inside.
2. Wash and rinse the broccoli florets then pat them dry.
3. Crack the eggs. Add almond flour to the liquid then season with salt and pepper.
4. Mix until incorporated.
5. Preheat an Air Fryer to 400°F (204°C).
6. Dip a broccoli floret in the coconut flour mixture then place in the Air Fryer.
7. Repeat with the remaining broccoli florets.
8. Cook the broccoli florets for 6 minutes. You may do this in several batches.
9. Once it is done, remove the fried broccoli popcorn from the Air Fryer then place on a serving dish.
10. Serve and enjoy immediately.

5 MINUTES

6 MINUTES

4

Marinated Portobello Mushroom

BASIC RECIPE

NUTRITION

alories 96 | Carbs 7.5g
at 7.9g | Protein 3.6g

DIRECTIONS

Clean and wash portable mushrooms and remove stems. Set aside.

In a bowl, mix the shallot, garlic, olive oil, and balsamic vinegar. Season with pepper, to taste.

Arrange portabello mushrooms, cap side up and brush with balsamic vinegar mixture.

5. Let it stand for at least 30 minutes.
6. Preheat your Air Fryer to 360°F.
7. Place marinated portabello mushroom on Air Fryer cooking basket. Cook for about 15- 20 minutes or until mushrooms are tender.
8. Serve and enjoy!

SHOPPING LIST

- 4 pcs. Portabello mushrooms
- 1 chopped shallot
- 1 teaspoon minced garlic
- 2 tbsps. Olive oil
- 2 tbsps. Balsamic vinegar
- Ground black pepper

15-20 MINUTES

4

30 MINUTES

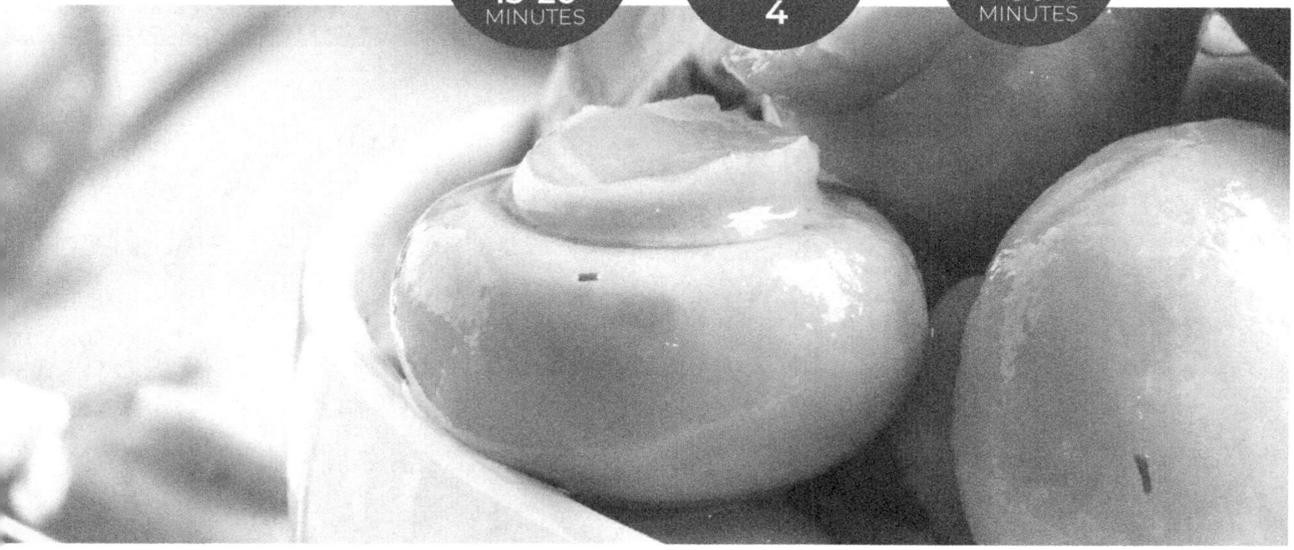

Fettuccini with Roasted Vegetables

INTERMEDIATE RECIPE

NUTRITION

Calories 330
Carbs 45.3g
Fat 12.4g
Protein 9.9g.

SHOPPING LIST

- 10 oz. spaghetti, cooked
- 1 eggplant, chopped
- 1 chopped bell pepper
- 1 zucchini, chopped
- 4 oz. halved grape tomatoes
- 1 teaspoon minced garlic
- 4 tbsps. Divided olive oil
- Kosher salt
- Ground black pepper
- 12 oz. can diced tomatoe
- ½ teaspoon dried basil
- ½ teaspoon dried oregano
- 1 teaspoon Spanish paprika
- 1 teaspoon brown sugar

DIRECTIONS

1. In a mixing bowl, combine eggplant, red bell pepper, zucchini, grape tomatoes, garlic, and 2 tablespoons olive oil.
2. Add some salt and pepper, to taste.
3. Preheat your Air Fryer to 390°F.
4. Place vegetable mixture in the Air Fryer cooking basket and cook for about 10-12 minutes, or until vegetables are tender.
5. Meanwhile, you can start preparing the tomato sauce.
6. In a saucepan, heat remaining 2 tablespoons olive oil.
7. Stir fry garlic for 2 minutes. Add diced tomatoes and simmer for 3 minutes.
8. Stir in basil, oregano, paprika, and brown sugar. Season with salt and pepper, to taste.
9. Let it cook for another 5-7 minutes. Once cooked, transfer the vegetables from Air
10. Fryer to a mixing bowl.
11. Add the cooked spaghetti and prepared a sauce. Toss to combine well.
12. Divide into 4 serving plates. Serve.

Cauliflower Florets in Tomato Puree

BASICE RECIPE

NUTRITION

Calories 276
Fat 21.8g
Protein 13.8g
Carbs 5.4g

30 MINUTES

20 MINUTES

2

SHOPPING LIST

- 2 c. cauliflower florets
- 3 teaspoon Granulated garlic
- ½ teaspoon salt
- ½ teaspoon coriander
- 2 c. water
- 3 eggs
- ½ teaspoon pepper
- ¼ c. grated Mozzarella cheese
- 3 tbsps. Tomato pure

DIRECTIONS

1. Place garlic, salt, and coriander in a container then pour water into it. Stir until the seasoning is completely dissolved.
2. Add the cauliflower florets to the brine then submerge for at least 30 minutes.
3. After 30 minutes, remove the cauliflower florets from the brine, then wash and rinse them. Pat them dry.
4. Preheat an Air Fryer to 400°F (204°C).
5. Crash the eggs and place them in a bowl.
6. Season with pepper then whisks until incorporated.
7. Dip a cauliflower floret in the egg then place in the air fryer. Repeat with the remaining cauliflower florets and egg.
8. Cook the cauliflower florets for 12 minutes or until lightly golden and the egg is curly.
9. Sprinkle grated Mozzarella cheese then drizzle tomato puree on top.
10. Cook the cauliflower florets again for another 5 minutes then remove from the Air Fryer.
11. Transfer to a serving dish then serve. Enjoy warm.

Fried Green Beans Garlic

BASIC RECIPE

DIRECTIONS

. Preheat an Air Fryer to 390°F (200°C).
. Place the chopped green beans in the Air Fryer then brush with butter.
. Sprinkle salt, garlic, and rosemary over the green beans, then cook for 5 minutes.
4. Once the green beans are done, remove them from the Air Fryer then place them on a serving dish. Serve and enjoy warm.

SHOPPING LIST

- ¾ c. chopped green beans
- 2 teaspoon Granulated garlic
- 2 tbsps. Rosemary
- ½ teaspoon salt
- 1 tablespoon vegan butter

NUTRITION

:alories 72
'at 6.3g
Protein 0.7g
Carbs 4.5g

5 MINUTES

5 MINUTES

2

Tender Potato Pancakes

BASIC RECIPE

5 MINUTES

12 MINUTES

4

DIRECTIONS

1. Peel your potatoes and shred them up.
2. Soak the shredded potatoes under cold water to remove starch.
3. Drain the potatoes.
4. Take a bowl and add eggs, milk, butter, garlic powder, salt, and pepper.
5. Add in flour.
6. Mix well. Add the shredded potatoes.
7. Pre-heat your air fryer to 390°F.
8. Add ¼ cup of the potato pancake batter to your cooking basket and cook for 12 minutes until the golden brown texture is seen.

NUTRITION

Calories 248
Carbs 33g
Fat 11g
Protein 6g

SHOPPING LIST

- 4 potatoes, peeled and cleaned
- 1 chopped onion
- 1 beaten egg
- ¼ c. oat milk
- 2 tbsps. Vegan butter
- ½ teaspoon garlic powde
- ¼ teaspoon salt
- 3 tbsps. All-purpose flour
- Pepper

Brussels Sprout & Cheese

ASIC RECIPE

5 MINUTES | 20 MINUTES | 2

NUTRITION

:alories 224 | Protein 10.1g
:at 18.1g | Carbs 4.5g

SHOPPING LIST

- ¾ c. Brussels sprouts
- 1 tablespoon extra virgin olive oil
- ¼ teaspoon salt
- Freshly ground black pepper
- ¼ c. grated Mozzarella cheese

DIRECTIONS

Cut the Brussels sprouts into halves then place in a bowl.
Drizzle extra virgin olive oil over the Brussels sprouts then sprinkle salt on top.
Toss to combine.
Preheat an Air Fryer to 375°F (191°C).
Transfer the seasoned Brussels sprouts to the Air Fryer then cook for 15 minutes.
After 15 minutes, open the Air Fryer and sprinkle grated Mozzarella cheese over the cooked Brussels sprouts.
Cook the Brussels sprouts in the Air Fryer for 5 minutes or until the Mozzarella cheese is melted.
Once it is done, remove it from the Air Fryer then transfer it to a serving dish.
Serve and enjoy

Zucchini, Tomato & Mozzarella Pie

INTERMEDIATE RECIPES

NUTRITION

Calories 195
Carbs 9.6g
Fat 10.4g
Protein 18.2g.

9-10 MINUTES

25 MINUTES

4

DIRECTIONS

1. Preheat the air fryer to 400°F.
2. Halve the zucchini and thinly cut lengthwise into strips
3. Apply pepper and salt for seasoning and allow to sit in a colander for 9-10 minutes.
4. Transfer to paper towels to drain. In an even layer, arrange the zucchini in a small baking dish and sprinkle with minced garlic and pepper.
5. Sprinkle with olive oil and top with the mozzarella slices, followed by the tomato slices.
6. Sprinkle with the chopped basil, sea salt, and pepper.
7. Place the pan in the basket and bake at 400°F for 25 minutes, until the cheese has melted.
8. Remove from the air fryer and let it sit for 10 minutes.
9. Serve warm and enjoy.

SHOPPING LIST

- 3 medium zucchinis
- Sea salt
- 5 minced cloves garlic
- Freshly ground pepper
- Olive oil
- 8 oz. sliced mozzarella
- 3 sliced vine-ripe or heirloom tomatoes
- Freshly chopped basil

Air fryer Cauliflower Rice

BASIC RECIPE

NUTRITION

Calories 67
Protein 3g
Fat 8g

SHOPPING LIST

- Round 1:
- Teaspoon Turmeric
- 1 c. Diced carrot
- ½ c. Diced onion
- 2 tablespoons Low-sodium soy sauce
- ½ block of extra firm tofu
- Round 2:
- ½ c. Frozen peas
- 2 minced garlic cloves
- ½ c. Chopped broccoli
- 1 tablespoon Minced ginger
- 1 tablespoon Rice vinegar
- 1 ½ teaspoon Toasted sesame oil
- 2 tablespoon Reduced-sodium soy sauce
- 3 c. Riced cauliflower

DIRECTIONS

1. Crumble tofu in a large bowl and toss with all the round one ingredient.
2. Preheat the air fryer oven to 370°F, place the baking dish in the air fryer oven cooking basket, set the temperature to 370°F, and set time to 10 minutes and cook 10 minutes, making sure to shake once.
3. In another bowl, toss ingredients from round 2 together.
4. Add round 2 mixture to air fryer and cook another 10 minutes, ensuring to shake 5 minutes in.

5 MINUTES

20 MINUTES

Garlic Butter Chicken

BASIC RECIPE

NUTRITION

Calories 641 | Total Carbs 2.36g | Protein 61.05g | Sodium 328mg
Total Fat 41.83g | Fiber 0.5g | Sugar 0.74g

SHOPPING LIST

- 1 tbsp olive oil
- 4 chicken breasts, boneless and skinless
- Salt and black pepper to taste
- 1 tsp paprika
- 4 tbsp melted butter
- 2 garlic cloves, minced
- 1 tsp Italian seasoning
- 1 tbsp chopped fresh parsley

DIRECTIONS

1. Heat the olive oil in a medium skillet, season the chicken with salt, black pepper, paprika, and sear the chicken in the oil on both sides until golden brown, 5 minutes.
2. Transfer to an 8-inch baking dish and set aside.
3. In a small bowl, mix the remaining ingredients and pour the mixture all over the chicken.
4. Insert the dripping pan onto the bottom of the air fryer oven and preheat at Bake mode at 340°F for 2 to 3 minutes.
5. Next, slide the cooking tray upside down onto the middle rack of the oven, place the dish on the tray and close the oven.
6. Set the timer for 16 minutes and press Start.
7. Cook until the timer reads to the end.
8. Remove the dish when ready and serve the chicken with sauce warm. Preheat an Air Fryer to 425°F (218°C). Arrange the spinach envelopes in the Air Fryer then cook for 12 minutes or until lightly golden brown.
9. Remove from the Air Fryer then serve warm.

Air Fried Carrots, Yellow Squash & Zucchini

INTERMEDIATE RECIPE

SHOPPING LIST

- 1 tablespoon Chopped tarragon leaves
- ½ teaspoon White pepper
- 1 teaspoon Salt
- 1 pound yellow squash
- 1 pound zucchini
- 6 teaspoon Olive oil
- ½ pound carrots

DIRECTIONS

1. Stem and root the end of squash and zucchini and cut in ¾-inch half-moons.
2. Peel and cut carrots into 1-inch cubes. Combine carrot cubes with 2 teaspoons of olive oil, tossing to combine.
3. Pour into the air fryer oven basket, set temperature to 400°F, and set time to 5 minutes.
4. As carrots cook, drizzle remaining olive oil over squash and zucchini pieces, then season with pepper and salt.
5. Toss well to coat. Add squash and zucchini when the timer for carrots goes off.
6. Cook 30 minutes, making sure to toss 2-3 times during the cooking process.
7. Once done, take out veggies and toss them with tarragon. Serve up warm.

5 MINUTES

35 MINUTES

4

NUTRITION

Calories 122

Fat 9g - Protein 6g

Brown Rice, Spinach & Tofu Frittata

INTERMEDIATE RECIPE

SHOPPING LIST

- ½ cup baby spinach, chopped
- ½ cup kale, chopped
- ½ onion, chopped
- ½ teaspoon turmeric
- 1 ¾ cups brown rice, cooked
- 1 flax egg (1 tablespoon flaxseed meal + 3
- tablespoon cold water) 1 package firm tofu
- 1 tablespoon olive oil
- 1 yellow pepper, chopped
- 2 tablespoons soy sauce
- 2 teaspoons arrowroot powder
- 2 teaspoons Dijon mustard
- 2/3 cup almond milk
- 3 big mushrooms, chopped
- 3 tablespoons nutritional yeast
- 4 cloves garlic, crushed
- 4 spring onions, chopped
- A handful of basil leaves, chopped

NUTRITION

Calories 226

Fat 8.05g - Protein 10.6

DIRECTIONS

1. Preheat the air fryer oven to 375°F. Grease a pan that will fit inside the air fryer oven.
2. Prepare the frittata crust by mixing the brown rice and flax egg.
3. Press the rice onto the baking dish until you form a crust. Brush with a little oil and cook for 10 minutes.
4. Meanwhile, heat olive oil in a skillet over medium flame and sauté the garlic and onions for 2 minutes.
5. Add the pepper and mushroom and continue stirring for 3 minutes.
6. Stir in the kale, spinach, spring onions, and basil. Remove from the pan and set aside.
7. In a food processor, pulse together the tofu, mustard, turmeric, soy sauce, nutritional yeast, vegan milk and arrowroot powder.
8. Pour in a mixing bowl and stir in the sautéed vegetables.
9. Pour the vegan frittata mixture over the rice crust and cook in the air fryer oven for 40 minutes.

5 MINUTES

55 MINUTES

4

Instant Brussels Sprout With Balsamic Oil

BASIC RECIPE

NUTRITION

Calories 82
Protein 1.5g
Fat 6.8g

DIRECTIONS

1. Preheat the air fryer oven for 5 minutes.
2. Mix all ingredients in a bowl until the
3. zucchini fries are well coated.
4. Place in the air fryer oven basket.
5. Close and cook for 15 minutes for 350°F.

SHOPPING LIST

- ¼ teaspoon salt
- 1 tablespoon balsamic vinegar
- 2 cups Brussels sprouts, halved
- Tablespoons olive oil

5 MINUTES

15 MINUTES

4

Cheesy Cauliflower Fritters

BASIC RECIPE

NUTRITION

Calories 209
Fat 17g
Protein 6g
Sugar 0.5

DIRECTIONS

1. Cut cauliflower up into florets. Wash well and pat dry.
2. Place into a food processor and pulse 20-30 seconds till it looks like rice.
3. Place cauliflower rice in a bowl and mix with pepper, salt, egg, cheeses, breadcrumbs, garlic, and scallions.
4. With hands, form 15 patties of the mixture.
5. Add more breadcrumbs if needed.
6. With olive oil, spritz patties, and place into your air fryer oven basket in a single layer.
7. Set the temperature to 390°f, and set time to 7 minutes, flipping after 7 minutes.

SHOPPING LIST

- ½ c. Chopped parsley
- 1 c. Italian breadcrumbs
- 1/3 c. Shredded mozzarella cheese
- 1/3 c. Shredded sharp cheddar cheese
- 1 egg
- 2 minced garlic cloves
- 3 chopped scallions
- 1 head of cauliflower
- pepper and salt to taste

10 MINUTES

7

8 MINUTES

Delicious Buttered Carrot-Zucchini with Mayo

BASIC RECIPE

NUTRITION

Calories 223 Protein 2.7g
Fat 17g Sugar 0.5

DIRECTIONS

1. Lightly grease the baking pan of the air fryer with cooking spray.
2. Add carrots. For 8 minutes, cook on 360°F
3. Add zucchini and continue cooking for another 5 minutes.
4. Meanwhile, in a bowl whisk well pepper, salt, horseradish, onion, mayonnaise, and water.
5. Pour into the pan of veggies. Toss well to coat. In a small bowl mix melted butter and bread crumbs. Sprinkle over veggies.
6. Pour into the oven rack/basket. Place the rack on the middle-shelf of the air fryer oven.
7. Set temperature to 490°f, and set time to 10 minutes until tops are lightly browned.
8. Serve and enjoy.

SHOPPING LIST

- 1 tablespoon grated onion
- 2 tablespoons butter, melted
- 1/2-pound carrots, sliced
- 1-1/2 zucchinis, sliced
- 1/4 cup water
- 1/4 cup mayonnaise
- 1/4 teaspoon prepared horseradish
- 1/4 teaspoon salt
- 1/4 teaspoon ground black pepper
- 1/4 cup Italian bread crumbs

Avocado Fries

BASICE RECIPE

NUTRITION

Calories 102
Fat 22g
Protein 9g
Sugar 1g

SHOPPING LIST

- 1 avocado
- ½ teaspoon Salt
- ½ c. Panko breadcrumbs
- Bean liquid (aquafaba) from a 15-ounce can
- of white or garbanzo beans

10 MINUTES

7 MINUTES

6

DIRECTIONS

1. Peel, pit, and slice up avocado.
2. Toss salt and breadcrumbs together in a bowl. Place aquafaba into another bowl.
3. Dredge slices of avocado first in aquafaba and then in panko, making sure you get an even coating.
4. Place coated avocado slices into a single layer in the air fryer oven basket.
5. Set temperature to 390°F, and set time to 5 minutes.
6. Serve with your favorite keto dipping sauce

Yummy Cheddar, Squash & Zucchini Casserole

INTERMEDIATE RECIPE

DIRECTIONS

1. Lightly grease the baking pan of the air fryer with cooking spray.
2. Add onion, zucchini, and yellow squash.
3. Cover pan with foil and for 15 minutes, cook at 360°F or until tender.
4. Stir in salt, sugar, egg, butter, baking mix, and cheddar cheese.
5. Mix well. Fold in crushed crackers. Top with bread crumbs.
6. Cook for 15 minutes at 390°F until tops are lightly browned.
7. Serve and enjoy.

SHOPPING LIST

- 1 egg
- 5 saltine crackers, or as needed, crushed
- 2 tablespoons bread crumbs
- 1/2-pound yellow squash, sliced
- 1/2-pound zucchini, sliced
- 1/2 cup shredded cheddar cheese
- 1-1/2 teaspoons white sugar
- 1/2 teaspoon salt
- 1/4 onion, diced
- 1/4 cup biscuit baking mix
- 1/4 cup butter

NUTRITION

Calories 285; Fat 20.5g; Protein 8.6g

5 MINUTES

30 MINUTES

4

Zucchini Parmesan Chips

BASIC RECIPE

DIRECTIONS

1. Use a very sharp knife or mandolin slicer to slice zucchini as thinly as you can.
2. Pat off extra moisture.
3. Beat egg with a pinch of pepper and salt and a bit of water.
4. Combine paprika, cheese, and breadcrumbs in a bowl.
5. Dip slices of zucchini into the egg mixture and then into breadcrumb mixture.
6. Press gently to coat.
7. With olive oil cooking spray, mist coated zucchini slices.
8. Place into your air fryer oven basket in a single layer.
9. Set temperature to 350°f, and set time to 8 minutes.
10. Sprinkle with salt and serve with salsa.

10 MINUTES

SHOPPING LIST

- ½ teaspoon Paprika
- ½ c. Grated parmesan cheese
- ½ c. Italian breadcrumbs
- 1 lightly beaten egg
- 2 thinly sliced zucchinis
- Salt and pepper to taste

NUTRITION

Calories 211; Protein 8g;
Fat 16g; Sugar 0g

8 MINUTES

10

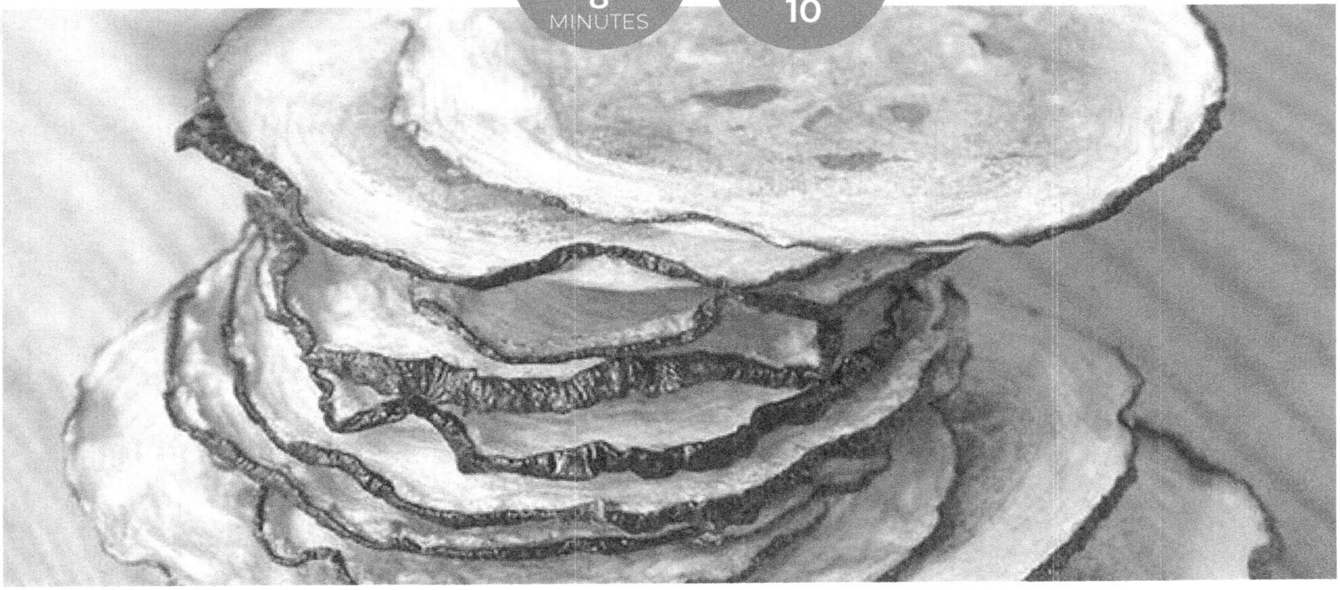

Jalapeño Cheese Balls

BASIC RECIPE

NUTRITION

Calories 96; Protein 4g;
Fat 6g; Sugar 0g

10 MINUTES

8 MINUTES

12

DIRECTIONS

1. In a medium bowl, combine the cream cheese, mozzarella, cheddar, and jalapeños.
2. Mix well. Form the cheese mixture into balls about an inch thick. Using a small ice cream scoop works well.
3. Arrange the cheese balls on a sheet pan and place them in the freezer for 15 minutes. This will help the cheese balls maintain their shape while frying.
4. Spray the air fryer oven basket with cooking oil.
5. Place the bread crumbs in a small bowl.
6. In another small bowl, beat the eggs. In a third small bowl, combine the flour with salt and pepper to taste, and mix well.
7. Remove the cheese balls from the freezer.
8. Dip the cheese balls in the flour, then the eggs, and then the bread crumbs.
9. Place the cheese balls in the air fryer. Spray with cooking oil. Set temperature to 360°F.
10. Cook for 8 minutes. Open the air fryer oven and flip the cheese balls. I recommend flipping them instead of shaking so the balls maintain their form.
11. Cook an additional 4 minutes. Cool before serving.

SHOPPING LIST

- 4 ounces cream cheese
- ⅓Cup shredded mozzarella cheese
- ⅓Cup shredded cheddar cheese
- 2 jalapeños, finely chopped
- ½ cup bread crumbs
- 2 eggs
- ½ cup all-purpose flour
- Salt
- Pepper
- Cooking oil

Crispy Roasted Broccoli

BASIC RECIPES

NUTRITION

Calories 96; Protein 7g;
Fat 1.3g; Sugar 4.5g

10 MINUTES

8 MINUTES

2

DIRECTIONS

1. Cut broccoli up into florets. Soak in a bowl of water with 2 teaspoons of salt for at least half an hour to remove impurities.
2. Take out broccoli florets from water and let drain. Wipe down thoroughly. Mix all other ingredients to create a marinade.
3. Toss broccoli florets in the marinade. Cover and chill for 15-30 minutes.
4. Preheat the air fryer oven to 390°F. Place marinated broccoli florets into the fryer basket, set the temperature to 350°F, and set the time to 10 minutes.
5. Florets will be crispy when done.

SHOPPING LIST

- ¼ teaspoon Masala
- ½ teaspoon Red chili powder
- ½ teaspoon Salt
- ¼ teaspoon Turmeric powder
- 1 tablespoon Chickpea flour
- 2 tablespoon Yogurt
- 1 pound broccoli

Creamy & Cheese Broccoli Bake

INTERMEDIATE RECIPE

2

NUTRITION

Calories 444; Protein 23g
Fat 22.3g;

SHOPPING LIST

- 1-pound fresh broccoli, coarsely chopped
- 2 tablespoons all-purpose flour
- Salt to taste
- 1 tablespoon dry bread crumbs, or to taste
- 1/2 large onion, coarsely chopped
- 1/2 (14 ounces) can evaporated milk, divided
- 1/2 cup cubed sharp cheddar cheese
- 1-1/2 teaspoons butter, or to taste
- 1/4 cup water
- cooking spray

DIRECTIONS

1. Lightly grease the baking pan of the air fryer with cooking spray.
2. Mix in half of the milk and flour in the pan and for 5 minutes, cook on 360°F.
3. Halfway through cooking time, mix well. Add broccoli and remaining milk.
4. Mix well and cook for another 5 minutes.
5. Stir in cheese and mix well until melted.
6. In a small bowl mix well, butter and bread crumbs.
7. Sprinkle on top of broccoli. Place the baking pan in the air fryer oven.
8. Cook for 20 minutes at 360°F until tops are lightly browned.
9. Serve and enjoy.

5 MINUTES

30 MINUTES

Jalapeno Egg Stuffed Avocado

BASIC RECIPE

NUTRITION

Net Carbs: 0.4g | Total Fat: 14.5g | Protein: 7.7g | Fiber: 2.1g
Calories: 175 | Saturated Fat: 3.6g | Carbs: 2.5g | Sugar: 1.4g

SHOPPING LIST

- 2 ripe avocados
- 2 tablespoons diced onion
- 2 tablespoons diced tomato
- 1-teaspoon diced cilantro
- 1-tablespoon lemon juice
- ¼ teaspoon salt
- ¼ teaspoon black pepper
- 4 eggs
- ¼ cups crumbled cottage cheese
- 1 green jalapeno

DIRECTIONS

1. Cut the avocados into halves then discard the seeds.
2. Crinkle aluminum foil under each avocado to keep the avocado from rolling then place on a cooking tray.
3. Combine diced onion, diced tomato, diced cilantro, lemon juice, salt, and pepper then mix well.
4. Fill each halved avocado with the vegetable mixture then drop an egg in it avocado. sprinkle crumbled cottage cheese on top then garnish with sliced jalapeno.
5. Next, set the drip pan at the bottom of the Air Fryer then selects the "Bake" menu.
6. Set the temperature to 350°F (177°C) and adjust the time to 5 minutes.
7. Press the "Start" button and wait until the Air Fryer indicates "Add Food".
8. Insert the cooking tray into the cooking chamber then put the cooking tray with avocados on it.
9. Let the Air Fryer Oven work and bake the avocados until it is done.
10. Serve and enjoy.

14 MINUTES

5 MINUTES

4

Nutty Vanilla Egg Tart

BASIC RECIPE

SHOPPING LIST

- 1-cup almond flour
- A pinch of salt
- ¾ cup butter
- 2 tablespoons cold water
- 4 eggs
- ½ cup monk fruits sweetener
- ¼ cup unsweetened almond milk
- 2 teaspoons vanilla
- ¼ cup chopped roasted almonds
- ¼ cup chopped roasted pecans
- ¼ cup chopped roasted walnuts

NUTRITION

Net Carbs: 1.2g
Calories: 256
Total Fat: 25.8g
Saturated Fat: 12g
Protein: 5.4g
Carbs: 2.3g
Fiber: 1.1 g
Sugar: 0.6g

24 MINUTES

30 MINUTES

8

DIRECTIONS

1. Place almond flour and salt in a mixing bowl then add ½ cup of butter to it.
2. Knead the flour and butter until becoming dough and add cold water if it is necessary.
3. Wrap the dough with plastic wrap then refrigerate it for approximately 15 minutes.
4. After 15 minutes, remove it from the fridge and roll it into a thin layer of dough.
5. Transfer the thin dough to a medium pie pan then press it.
6. Next, set the drip pan at the bottom of the Air Fryer then select the "Bake" menu.
7. Set the temperature to 325°F (163°C) and adjust the time to 10 minutes.
8. Press the "Start" button and wait until the Air Fryer indicates "Add Food".
9. Insert the cooking tray into the cooking chamber then place the pie pan on it.
10. Let the Air Fryer Oven work and cook the piecrust until done.
11. In the meantime, crack the eggs then place them in a bowl.
12. Add the remaining butter to the eggs together with monk fruits sweetener, almond milk, and vanilla.
13. Using a hand mixer beat the filling ingredients until smooth

then set aside.

14. Once the piecrust is done, take it out of the Air Fryer and let it cool for a few minutes.
15. When the piecrust is cool enough, pour the filling mixture into the piecrust and spread it evenly.
16. Sprinkle almonds, pecans, and walnuts on top then set aside.
17. Select the "Bake" menu and set the temperature to 325°F (163°C) and the time to 20 minutes.
18. Once the Air Fryer indicates "Add Food", return the pie to the cooking chamber and cook until the filling is firm.
19. Remove the pie from the Air Fryer and serve. to set the temperature at 390°F.
20. Press the "Start/Pause" button to start. When the unit beeps to show that it is preheated, open the lid.
21. Arrange the veggie mixture in "Air Fry Basket" and insert it in the oven. Serve hot.

Coconut Battered Cauliflower Bites

BASIC RECIPE

SHOPPING LIST

- Salt and pepper to taste
- 1 flax egg (1 tablespoon flaxseed meal + 3
- tablespoon water) 1 small cauliflower, cut
- into florets
- 1 teaspoon mixed spice
- ½ teaspoon mustard powder
- 2 tablespoons maple syrup
- 1 clove of garlic, minced
- 2 tablespoonssoy sauce
- 1/3 cupoatsflour
- 1/3 cup plain flour
- 1/3 cup desiccated coconut

DIRECTIONS

1. Preheat the air fryer oven to 400°F. In a mixing bowl, mix oats, flour, and desiccated coconut.
2. Season with salt and pepper to taste. Set aside.
3. In another bowl, place the flax egg and add a pinch of salt to taste. Set aside.
4. Season the cauliflower with mixed spice and mustard powder. Dredge the florets in the flax egg first then in the flour mixture.
5. Place inside the air fryer oven and cook for 15 minutes.
6. Meanwhile, place the maple syrup, garlic, and soy sauce in a sauce pan and heat over medium flame.
7. Bring to a boil and adjust the heat to low until the sauce thickens.
8. After 15 minutes, take out the florets from the air fryer and place them in the saucepan.
9. Toss to coat the florets and place inside the air fryer and cook for another 5 minutes.

5 MINUTES

20 MINUTES

4

NUTRITION

Calories 154

Protein 4.69g

Fat 2.3g

Crispy Jalapeno Coins

BASIC RECIPE

NUTRITION

Calories 128
Protein 7g
Fat 8g
Sugar 0g

DIRECTIONS

1. Ensure your air fryer oven is preheated to 400°F.
2. Mix all dry ingredients.
3. Pat jalapeno slices dry. Dip coins into the egg wash and then into a dry mixture.
4. Toss to thoroughly coat.
5. Add coated jalapeno slices to the air fryer basket in a singular layer. Spray with olive oil.
6. Set temperature to 350°F, and set time to 5 minutes. Cook just till crispy.

SHOPPING LIST

- 1 egg
- 2-3 tablespoon Coconut flour
- 1 sliced and seeded jalapeno
- Pinch of garlic powder
- Pinch of onion powder
- Pinch of Cajun seasoning (optional)
- Pinch of pepper and salt

10 MINUTES

5 MINUTES

2

Buffalo Cauliflower

BASIC RECIPE

NUTRITION

Calories 194
Protein 10g
Fat 17g
Sugar 3

DIRECTIONS

Melt butter in microwave and whisk in buffalo sauce.

Dip each cauliflower floret into buffalo the mixture, ensuring it gets coated well.

Hold over a bowl till floret is done dripping.

Mix breadcrumbs with salt.

Dredge dipped florets into breadcrumbs and place them into the air fryer basket.

6. Set temperature to 350°F, and set time to 15 minutes.
7. When slightly browned, they are ready to eat!
8. Serve with your favorite keto dipping sauce.

SHOPPING LIST

- Cauliflower:
- 1 c. Panko breadcrumbs
- 1 teaspoon Salt
- 4 c. Cauliflower florets
Buffalo coating:
- ¼ c. Vegan buffalo sauce
- ¼ c. Melted vegan butter

15 MINUTES

2

5 MINUTES

Smoked Beef Burgers

BASIC RECIPE

NUTRITION

167 Calories
5.5g Fat
1.4g Carbs
26.4g Protein
0g Sugars
0.4g Fiber

DIRECTIONS

1. Mix all of the above ingredients in a bowl; knead until everything is well incorporated.
2. Shape the mixture into four patties. Next, make a shallow dip in the center of each patty to prevent them puffing up during airfrying.
3. Spritz the patties on all sides using a nonstick cooking spray. Cook approximately 12 minutes at 360°F.
4. Verify that it is well cooked, an instant read thermometer should read 160°F.

Bon appétit!

10 MINUTES

10 MINUTES

4

SHOPPING LIST

- 1 ¼ pounds lean ground beef
- 1 tablespoon soy sauce
- 1 teaspoon Dijon mustarc
- A few dashes of liquid smoke
- 1 teaspoon shallot powder
- 1 clove garlic, minced
- 1/2 teaspoon cumin powder
- 1/4 cup scallions, minced
- 1/3 teaspoon sea salt flakes
- 1/3 teaspoon freshly cracked mixed
- peppercorns
- 1 teaspoon celery seeds
- 1 teaspoon parsley flakes

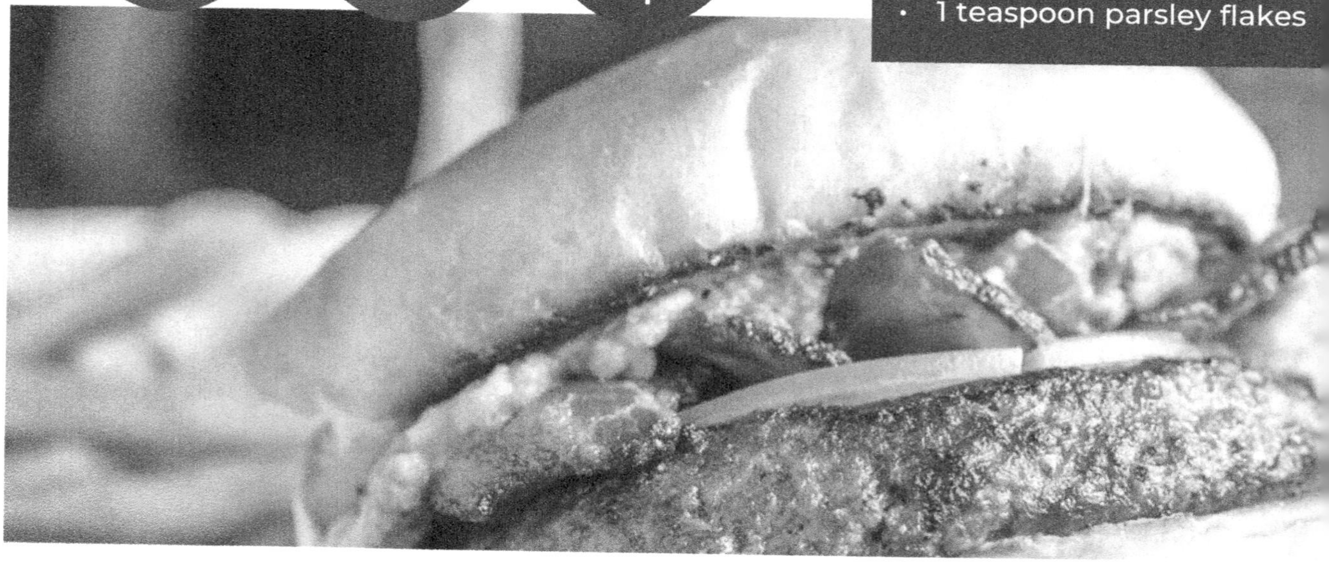

Spicy Holiday Roast Beef

BASICE RECIPE

NUTRITION

243 Calories
10.6g Fat
0.4g Carbs
34.5g Protein

SHOPPING LIST

- 2 pounds roast beef, at room temperature
- 2 tablespoons extra-virgin olive oil
- 1 teaspoon sea salt flakes
- 1 teaspoon black pepper, preferably freshly
- ground
- 1 teaspoon smoked paprika
- A few dashes of liquid smoke
- 2 jalapeño peppers, thinly sliced

DIRECTIONS

1. Start by preheating the Air Fryer to 330⁰F. Then, pat the roast dry using kitchen towels. Rub with extra-virgin olive oil and all seasonings along with liquid smoke.
2. Roast for 30 minutes in the preheated Air Fryer; then, pause the machine and turn the roast over; roast for additional 15 minutes.
3. Check for doneness using a meat thermometer and serve sprinkled with sliced jalapeños. Bon appétit!

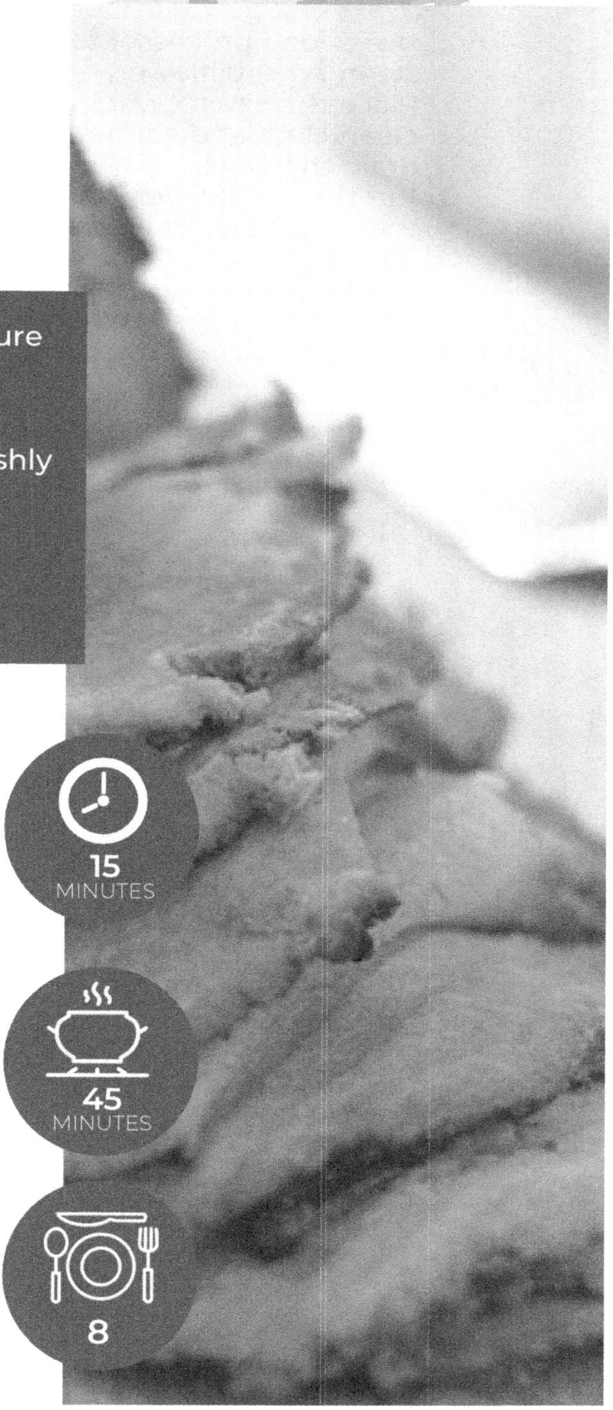

Cauliflower Tots

BASIC RECIPE

DIRECTIONS

1. Use a food processor for steamed cauliflower.
2. Place the cauliflower rice on a clean cloth and squeeze it to drain the water.
3. Put the cauliflower with the egg, cheddar cheese, parmesan, panko and chives in a large bowl and mix until everything is well combined.
4. Season with salt and pepper.
5. Pour about 1 tablespoon of the mixture with a spoon and roll with your hands.
6. Work in batches, place them in a single layer in the basket of the air fryer and cook at 375^{0}F until the containers are golden.
7. Place in a small bowl and stir.
8. Serve the cauliflower tots.

SHOPPING LIST

- Cooking spray
- 4 cup Cauliflower florets, steamed (about
- 1/2 large cauliflower)
- 1 large Egg, lightly beaten
- 1 cup Shredded cheddar
- 1 cup freshly grated Parmesan
- 2/3 cup Panko breadcrumbs
- 2 tablespoons freshly chopped chives
- Kosher salt
- Freshly Ground black pepper

NUTRITION

Calories 115
Total Fat 4.8g
Total Carbohydrate 6.3g
Protein 12.7g

10 MINUTES
15 MINUTES
6

Apple Chips

BASIC RECIPE

DIRECTIONS

1. In a large bowl, mix the apples with cinnamon and stevia.
2. Work in batches, placing the apples in one layer in the air fryer basket (a small overlap is fine).
3. Cook for about 12 minutes at 350^{0}F and turn every 4 minutes.

NUTRITION

Calories 117
Total Fat 0.4g
Total Carbohydrate 31.3g
Protein 0.6g

5 MINUTES

SHOPPING LIST

- 4 Apples, thinly sliced
- 2 teaspoons Stevia
- 1 teaspoon Cinnamon

24 MINUTES

4

Crispy Avocado Fries

BASIC RECIPE

NUTRITION

Calories 330
Total Fat 23.2g
Total Carbohydrate 26.6g
Protein 7.8g

DIRECTIONS

1. Combine panko, garlic powder and paprika in a flat bowl.
2. Put the coconut flour in another flat bowl and a third flat bowl, beat the eggs, dip the avocado slices in the flour, then the egg, then the panko mixture until they are completely covered.
3. Place in the fryer, fry at 400°F for 10 minutes and serve.

SHOPPING LIST

- 1 cup Panko breadcrumbs
- 1 teaspoon Garlic powder
- 1 teaspoon Paprika
- 1 cup Coconut flour
- 2 Large eggs
- 2 Avocados, sliced

5 MINUTES

10 MINUTES

4

Coconut Sweet Potatoes

BASIC RECIPES

NUTRITION

Calories 228 | Total Carbohydrate 29.1g
Total Fat 9.9g | Protein 5.2g

10 MINUTES | 20 MINUTES | 4

DIRECTIONS

1. Preheat the fryer to 200°C. Spray the basket with an oil spray.
2. Combine the coconut flakes, panko, salt, paprika, garlic powder and pepper in a bowl.
3. Beat the egg in another bowl. Leave aside.
4. Dry the sweet potatoes with a paper towel.
5. First rinse each sweet potato in the egg and then in the breadcrumb mixture until it is completely covered.
6. Place them in the air fryer and put the sweet potatoes in the air fryer without overloading them.
7. Let it cook for about 5 minutes until everything is golden and golden. Repeat with the remaining sweet potatoes.
8. Serve with your favorite sauce and enjoy!

SHOPPING LIST

- ½ cup unsweetened coconut flakes
- ½ cup Panko bread crumbs
- ½ teaspoon Salt
- ½ teaspoon Paprika
- ½ teaspoon Garlic powder
- ¼ teaspoon Pepper
- 1 lb. Sweet potatoes, peeled, cut into length
- wise
- 1 Egg

Garlic Chicken Wings

INTERMEDIATE RECIPE

4

5
MINUTES

20
MINUTES

NUTRITION

Calories 125
Total Fat 5.8g
Total Carbohydrate 0.8g
Protein 16.6g

SHOPPING LIST

- 1- 1/2 lbs. Chicken wings
- ¼ cup Coconut flour
- 3 cloves Garlic
- 1 tablespoon butter
- 1/2 teaspoon salt
- 1 teaspoon red pepper flakes

DIRECTIONS

1. Preheat the air fryer for a few minutes.
2. Place the coconut flour in a large zipped plastic bag and add wings to the bag. Shake until the wings are evenly covered with coconut flour.
3. Grease the basket with a little oil (do not use cooking spray!) And place the wings in the basket. Shake off excess coconut flour while doing this, being careful not to stack them.
4. If necessary, cook in batches and bake at 360°F for 12 minutes. Turn and cook for another 12 minutes.
5. Raise the temperature to 400°F and bake for another 5-6 minutes to make it crispy.
6. Garlic and microwave for 30 seconds or until melted.
7. Add the season with a pinch of salt and red pepper.
8. Mix the wings in the sauce and serve.

Buns with Carrots and Nuts

INTERMEDIATE RECIPE

NUTRITION

Calories 195
Carbs 24.25g
Sugar 15.15g
Fat 11.04g
Protein 2.22g
Cholesterol 67mg

SHOPPING LIST

- ½ cup whole-grain flour
- ¼ cup of sugar,
- ½ teaspoon baking soda
- ¼ teaspoon cinnamon,
- ⅛ Teaspoon nutmeg
- ½ cup grated carrots
- 2 tbsps. chopped walnuts
- 2 tbsps. grated coconut,
- 2 tbsps. golden raisins
- 1 egg,
- 1 tablespoon milk,
- ½ teaspoon vanilla essence,
- ¼ cupapplesauce

DIRECTIONS

1. Preheat the fryer to a temperature of 350°F.
2. Grease the bottom of 4 muffin molds or glass cups for custard, or a magazine with muffin papers.
3. Combine flour, sugar, baking soda, cinnamon, and nutmeg in a medium bowl.
4. Add carrots, nuts, coconut, and raisins to the flour mixture.
5. Beat together the egg, milk, and vanilla in a small bowl.
6. Add the applesauce. Put the flour mixture and stir until well incorporated.
7. Fill the prepared molds or cups with an equal amount of dough (1/3 cup) and then put them inside the basket.
8. Cook for 15 minutes, then let them cool in the molds for 5 minutes before removing.

5 MINUTES

20 MINUTES

4

Pine Skewers Aceto Reduction

BASIC RECIPE

SHOPPING LIST

- 1 small can of pineapple in its juice
- Necessary quantity peeled prawns
- Skewers sticks
- For the sauce:
- 150 ml of balsamic aceto
- 120g of sugar

NUTRITION

Calories 226g
Carbs 36g
Cholesterol 156mg
Fat 2g
Proteins: 16g

DIRECTIONS

1. Open a small can of pineapple in its juice and drain well.
2. Cut the pineapple slices into four parts and set them aside.
3. Peel the prawns and take out the tail.
4. Preheat the air fryer at 180°C temperature for a few minutes and put the skewers in the basket.
5. Program the timer about 10 minutes at 180°C.
6. To prepare the balsamic Aceto sauce: place the Aceto and sugar in a small pot. Reduce over low heat until it thickens but without letting caramel.
7. Let stand until it cools. then set aside.
8. Once the piecrust is done, take it out of the Air Fryer and let it cool for a few minutes.
9. When the piecrust is cool enough, pour the filling mixture into the piecrust and spread it evenly.
10. Sprinkle almonds, pecans, and walnuts on top then set aside.
11. Select the "Bake" menu and set the temperature to 325°F (163°C) and the time to 20 minutes.
12. Once the Air Fryer indicates "Add

5 MINUTES

15 MINUTES

2

Food", return the pie to the cooking chamber and cook until the filling is firm.

13. Remove the pie from the Air Fryer and serve. to set the the temperature at 390°F.
14. Press the "Start/Pause" button to start. When the unit beeps to show that it is preheated, open the lid.
15. Arrange the veggie mixture in "Air Fry Basket" and insert in the oven. Serve hot.

Mini Burgers

BASIC RECIPE

SHOPPING LIST

- 500g ground beef
- Salt
- Ground pepper
- Garlic powder
- Fresh parsley
- Spices
- 1 egg
- 1 tablespoon Grated bread
- Mini bread for burgers

DIRECTIONS

1. Dress the meat of the hamburgers.
2. Add some salt to the ground beef, some ground pepper, garlic powder, a tablespoon of chopped fresh parsley, a teaspoon of spices.
3. Now, throw an egg and one or two teaspoons of breadcrumbs, so that the meat becomes more consistent. Stir all ingredients well until everything is integrated

NUTRITION

Calories 136g
Fat 3g
Carbs 25g
Proteins: 12g
Cholesterol 169mg

5 MINUTES

25 MINUTES

4

Chicken Sandwich

INTERMEDIATE RECIPE

NUTRITION

Calories 215
Carbs 38.7g
Assume: 0g
Fat 29.4g
Protein 24.1g
Cholesterol 60.1mg

SHOPPING LIST

- 2 cloves garlic
- Fresh parsley leaves
- 500g chopped breast
- 1 teaspoon Salt
- Pepper
- 1 egg l
- 50g milk
- 50g cheese spread
- 14-16 slices sliced bread
- 7-8 slices semi-cured cheese

DIRECTIONS

1. Chop the garlic and parsley.
2. Add the rest in pieces, salt, and pepper add the rest of the ingredients and spread slices!
3. Spread the paste on all the slices, cover half with a slice of cheese, and cover with another slice, cut into triangles and there are two options, pass them by egg and breadcrumbs
4. Preheat the 220°C air fryer, about 8 or 10 minutes, until the bread becomes colored.

5 MINUTES

15 MINUTES

2

Potato Balls Stuffed with Ham & Cheese From The air Fryer

INTERMEDIATE RECIPE

NUTRITION

Calories 224
Carbs 19g
Sugar 1g
Fat 14g
Protein 4g
Cholesterol 0mg

DIRECTIONS

. Peel the potatoes and cut them into quarters.
. Put in a pot with water and bring to the fire, let cook until tender.
. Drain and squeeze with a fork until the potatoes are made dough and season.
. Add the ham and cheese. Let's link everything.
. Make balls and pass through the flour. Spray with oil and go to the basket of the air fryer. Select 20 minutes, 200ºC for each batch of balls you put. Do not pile up because they would break down.
6. From time to time remove from the basket so that they are made on all sides, you have to shake the basket so that the balls roll a little and serve.

SHOPPING LIST

- 4 potatoes
- 100g cooked ham
- 100g of grated or grated cheese
- Salt
- Ground pepper
- Flour
- Oil

5 MINUTES

25

4 MINUTES

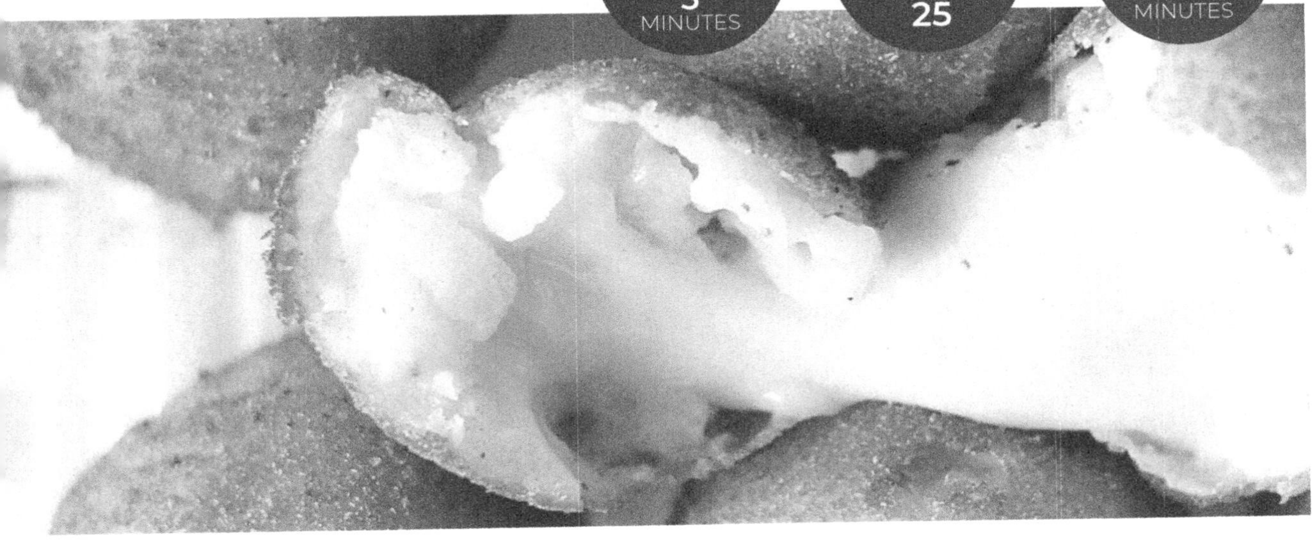

T-Bone Steak Santa Maria

EXPERT RECIPE

NUTRITION

Calories 115
Carbs 1.8g
Fat 2.6g

DIRECTIONS

1. Select Preheat in the air fryer and press
2. Start/Pause. Mix the seasonings and sprinkle on the steak.
3. Spray olive oil on the steak.
4. Place the fillet in the preheated air fryer, select Steak, and press Start/Pause.
5. Remove the fillet from the air fryer when finished.
6. Let stand for 10 minutes before cutting and serving.

SHOPPING LIST

- 2g of salt
- 2g black pepper
- 2g garlic powder
- 2g onion powder
- 2g dried oregano
- A pinch of dried rosemary
- A pinch of cayenne
- A pinch of dried sage
- 1 rib eye boneless
- 15 ml of olive oil

5 MINUTES

15 MINUTES

2

Steak with Chimichurri

EXPERT RECIPE

NUTRITION

Calories 333 | Carbs 4g | Sugar 1g
Fat 20g | Protein 34g | Cholesterol 104mg

SHOPPING LIST

- 12 ml of vegetable oil,
- 16 oz. Steak
- Salt and pepper to taste
- 60 ml of extra virgin olive oil
- 20g fresh basil,
- 20g coriander
- 20g parsley
- 4 anchovy fillets,
- 1 small shallot
- 2 cloves garlic, peeled
- 1 lemon, juiced
- A pinch of crushed red pepper

DIRECTIONS

1. Combine all the ingredients of the chimichurri sauce in a blender and mix until you reach the desired consistency.
2. Preheat the air fryer by pressing Start/ Pause Rub vegetable oil in the fryer on the steak and season with salt and pepper.
3. Place the fillet in the preheated air fryer. Select Steak, set the time to 6 minutes (so that it is half cooked), and press Start/Pause.
4. Allow the steak to rest for 5 minutes when finished.
5. Finally, cover with chimichurri sauce and serve.

Flank Steak with Balsamic Mustard

INTERMEDIATE RECIPE

DIRECTIONS

1. Mix olive oil, balsamic vinegar, and mustard.
2. Mix them together to create a marinade. Put the steak directly in the marinade.
3. Cover with plastic wrap and marinate in the fridge for 2 hours or at night.
4. Remove from the refrigerator and let it reach room temperature.
5. Preheat the air fryer by pressing Start/Pause.
6. Place the fillet in the preheated air fryer, select Fillet, and press Start/Pause. Cut the steak at an angle through the muscle.
7. Season with salt and pepper and decorate with basil to serve.

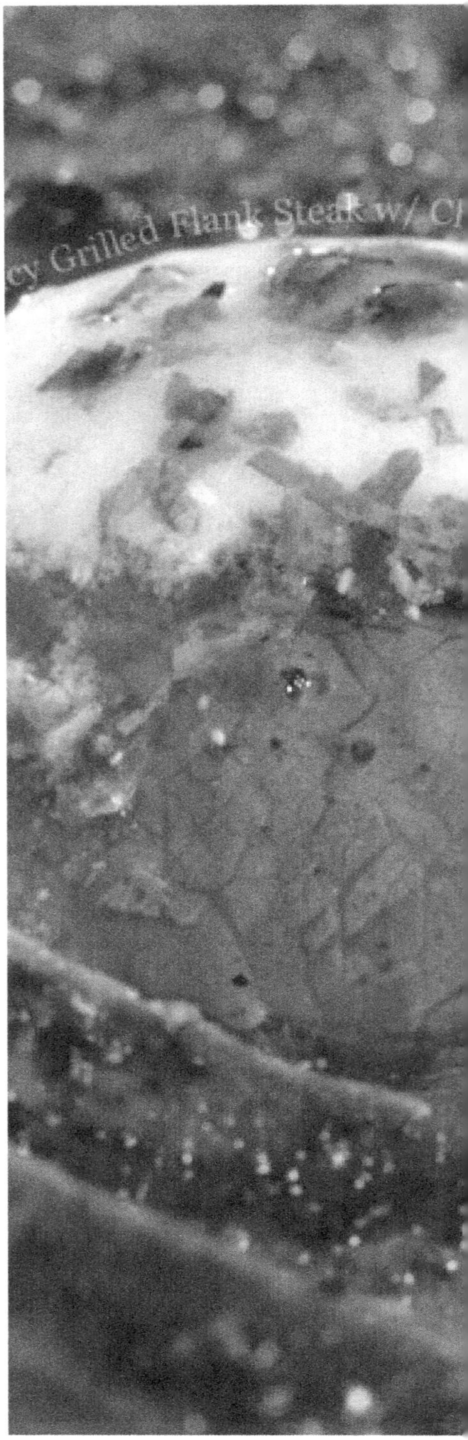

SHOPPING LIST

- 60 ml of olive oil
- 60 ml balsamic vinegar
- 36g Dijon mustard
- 16 oz. flank steak
- Salt and pepper to taste
- 4 basil leaves, sliced

NUTRITION

Calories 275
Carbs 18.8g
Sugar 6g
Fat 6.1g
Protein 29.5g

10 MINUTES

2H15 MINUTES

3

Italian Meatballs

INTERMEDIATE RECIPE

5 MINUTES

DIRECTIONS

1. Mix ground meat, breadcrumbs, eggs, spices, salt, pepper, and Parmesan. Create small balls with the meat mixture.
2. Place them in the refrigerator for 10 minutes.
3. Select Preheat in the air fryer and press Start/ Pause.
4. Remove the meatballs from the refrigerator and place them in the baskets of the preheated air fryer.
5. Spray the meatballs with oil spray and cook at 205°C for 8 minutes. Serve with marinara sauce and grated Parmesan cheese.

SHOPPING LIST

- 227g ground beef
- 28g of breadcrumbs
- 30 ml of milk
- 1 egg
- 3g garlic powder
- 2g onion powder
- 2g dried oregano
- 2g dried parsley
- Salt and pepper to taste,
- 15g grated Parmesan cheese, Spray oil

NUTRITION

Calories 286
Fat 22.21g
Carbs 18.1g
Protein 14.40g
Sugar 3.47g
Cholesterol 66mg

25 MINUTES

4

Peppers Stuffed with Potato Omele

INTERMEDIATE RECIPE

NUTRITION

Calories 133 | Carbs 17g | Sugar 0g
Fat 5g | Protein 5g | Cholesterol 50 mg

SHOPPING LIST

- 2 large peppers (green, rec
- 2 medium potatoes
- 1 egg
- 1 tablespoon olive oil
- Salt

15 MINUTES | 25 MINUTES | 2

DIRECTIONS

1. Preheat the air fryer for about 4 minutes at 180ºC.
2. While heating, peel and cut the potatoes as for tortillas.
3. Go through plenty of water and dry thoroughly.
4. Spray the cut potatoes with a little olive oil and place them in the fryer basket. Insert the basket in the air fryer and set the timer to about 12 minutes to 180ºC
5. Stir the potatoes halfway through cooking temperature.
6. While the potatoes are cooking, clean the peppers, cut the tops, and remove all the seeds. Spray the peppers with olive oil and lightly salt them.
7. When the potatoes are ready, salt them. Beat the egg and mix it with the potatoes.
8. Fill the peppers with this mixture and put them in the basket
9. Enter it again in the air fryer and program for about 7 minutes at 200ºC.

Longaniza Skewers

INTERMEDIATE RECIPES

NUTRITION

Calories 273 Carbs 1.12g Sugar 0g
Fat 29.96g Protein 14.46g

10 MINUTES

25 MINUTES

4

DIRECTIONS

1. Preheat the air fryer. Set the time of 5 minutes and the temperature to 200ºC.
2. At the end of the time, the air fryer will turn off.
3. Cut the sausages into thick slices with about 2 cm. Then season with salt and pepper.
4. Assemble the skewers alternating slices of sausage, peppers, and onions to finish all the ingredients.
5. Let the skewers with about 12 cm to fit in the basket of the air fryer. Cut the excess with kitchen scissors.
6. Brush with olive oil and set aside. Organize the skewers in the basket of the air fryer. Set the time of 20 minutes and press the power button.
7. After ready, transfer to a plate and serve.

SHOPPING LIST

- 4 fresh Tuscan sausages
- 2 peppers cut into squares
- 1 onion, cut into large cubes
- Coarse salt and pepper to taste
- 2 tbsps. of brush oil
- Wooden skewers

Eggplant Milanese

BASIC RECIPE

Servings: 2

5 MINUTES

40 MINUTES

NUTRITION

Calories 103 | Carbs 11.61g | Sugar 2.45
Fat 5.61g | Protein 2.4g | Cholesterol 14mg

SHOPPING LIST

- 1 medium eggplant
- 1 tablespoon of vinegar
- 2 lightly beaten whole eggs
- 1 cup of tea flour
- 1 ½ cup breadcrumbs

DIRECTIONS

1. Wash the eggplants and cut into slices of 1 cm maximum thickness, place the slices in a bowl with water and vinegar and let them soak for at least 15 minutes.
2. Preheat the air fryer. Set the time of 5 minutes and the temperature to 200^{0}F.
3. Remove water from eggplant slices and place on a roasting pan, sprinkle salt to taste. Pass each slice through the flour, then through the beaten egg and finally in breadcrumbs and squeezing the fingers and hands, so they remain very compact.
4. Place the eggplant slices in the basket of the air fryer and set the timer for 18 minutes and press the power button.
5. Open the time in half to see if the weather needs an adjustment because the eggplants should be crispy on the outside and soft on the inside.

Perfect Cinnamon Toast

INTERMEDIATE RECIPE

NUTRITION

Calories 124 Protein 0g
Fat 2g Sugar 4g

SHOPPING LIST

- 2 teaspoon pepper
- 1 ½ teaspoon vanilla extract
- 1 ½ teaspoon cinnamon
- ½ C. sweetener of choice
- 1 C. coconut oil
- 12 slices whole-wheat bread

DIRECTIONS

Melt coconut oil and mix with sweetener until it dissolves.
Mix remaining ingredients minus bread till just incorporated.

Spread mixture onto bread, covering all areas.

Pour the coated pieces of bread into the Oven rack/basket.
Place the Rack on the middle-shelf of the Cuisinart Air Fryer Oven. Set temperature to 400°F, and set time to 5 minutes.

Remove and cut diagonally. Enjoy!

10 MINUTES

5 MINUTES

6

Crispy Cauliflower Poppers

BASIC RECIPE

SHOPPING LIST

- 1 egg white
- 1½ tablespoons ketchup
- 1 tablespoon hot sauce
- 1/3 cup panko breadcrumbs
- 2 cups cauliflower florets

NUTRITION

Calories 55
Total Fat 0.7 g
Saturated Fat 0.3g
Cholesterol 0 mg
Sodium 181 mg
Total Carbs 5.6 g
Fiber 1.3 g
Sugar 2.6 g
Protein 2.3

DIRECTIONS

1. In a shallow bowl, mix the egg white, ketchup, and hot sauce.
2. In another bowl, place the breadcrumbs.
3. Dip the cauliflower florets in a ketchup mixture and then coat with the breadcrumbs.
4. Press "Power Button" of Air Fry Oven and turn the dial to select the "Air Fry" mode.
5. Press the Time button and again turn the dial to set the cooking time to 20 minutes.
6. Now push the Temp button and rotate the dial to set the temperature at 320°F.
7. Press the "Start/Pause" button to start.
8. When the unit beeps to show that it is preheated, open the lid.
9. Arrange the cauliflower florets in "Air Fry Basket" and insert in the oven.
10. Toss the cauliflower florets once halfway through.
11. Serve warm.

10 MINUTES

20 MINUTES

4

Broccoli Poppers

BASIC RECIPE

SHOPPING LIST

- 2 tablespoons plain yogurt
- ½ teaspoon red chili powder
- ¼ teaspoon ground cumin
- ¼ teaspoon ground turmeric
- Salt to taste
- 1 lb. broccoli, cut into small florets
- 2 tablespoons chickpea flour

DIRECTIONS

In a bowl, mix the yogurt, chickpea flour and spices.

Add the broccoli and coat with marinade generously.

Refrigerate for about 20 minutes.

Press "Power Button" of Air Fry Oven and turn the dial to select the "Air Fry" mode.

Press the Time button and again turn the dial to set the cooking time to 10 minutes.

Now push the Temp button and rotate the dial to set the temperature at 400°F.

Press the "Start/Pause" button to start.

When the unit beeps to show that it is preheated, open the lid.

Arrange the broccoli florets in "Air Fry Basket" and insert in the oven.

).Toss the broccoli florets once halfway through.

1. Serve warm.

NUTRITION

alories 69

otal Fat 0.9 g

aturated Fat 0.1 g

holesterol 0 mg

odium 87 mg

Total Carbs 12.2 g

Fiber 4.2 g

Sugar 3.2 g

Protein 4.9 g

15 MINUTES

10 MINUTES

4

Cheesy Broccoli Bites

BASIC RECIPE

NUTRITION

Calories 153 | Saturated Fat 4.5g | Sodium 172 mg | Fiber 0.5 g | Protein 7.1 g
Total Fat 8.2 g | Cholesterol 52 mg | Total Carbs 4 g | Sugar 0.5 g

DIRECTIONS

1. In a food processor, add the broccoli and pulse until finely crumbled.
2. In a large bowl, mix the broccoli, and remaining ingredients.
3. Make small equal-sized balls from the mixture.
4. Press "Power Button" of Air Fry Oven and turn the dial to select the "Air Fry" mode.
5. Press the Time button and again turn the dial to set the cooking time to 12 minutes.
6. Now push the Temp button and rotate the dial to set the temperature at 350°F.
7. Press the "Start/Pause" button to start.
8. When the unit beeps to show that it is preheated, open the lid.
9. Arrange the broccoli balls in "Air Fry Basket" and insert in the oven.
10. Serve warm.

SHOPPING LIST

- 1 cup broccoli florets
- 1 egg, beaten
- ¾ cup cheddar cheese grated
- 2 tablespoons Parmesan cheese, grated
- ¾ cup panko breadcrumbs
- Salt and freshly ground black pepper, as needed

15 MINUTES

12 MINUTES

5

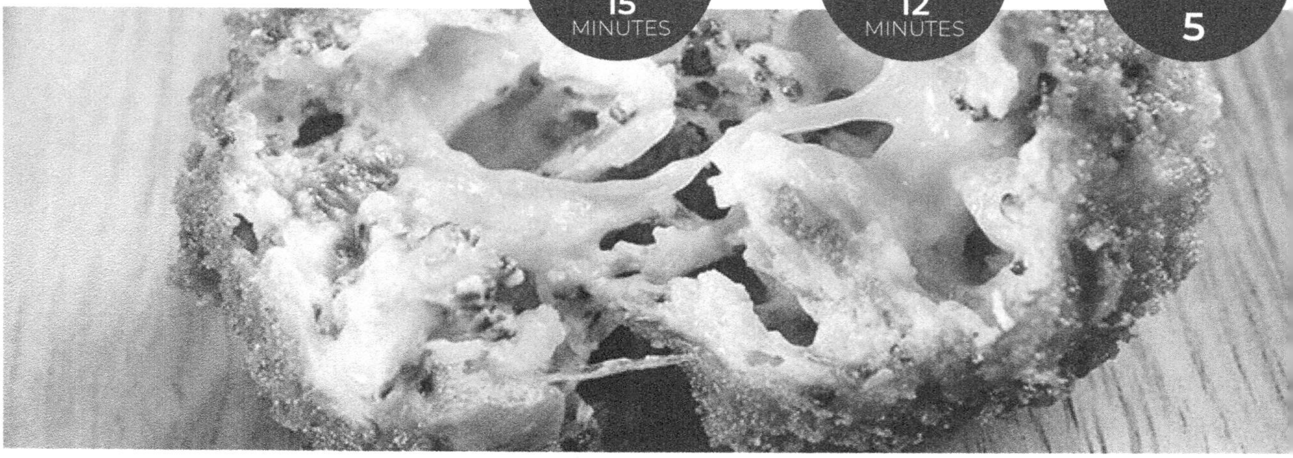

Easy Baked Chocolate Mug Cake

INTERMEDIATE RECIPE

NUTRITION

Calories 744
Protein 13.9g
Fat 69.7g
Sugar 4g

DIRECTIONS

1. Preheat the Cuisinart Air Fryer Oven for 5 minutes.
2. In a bowl, combine all ingredients.
3. Use a hand mixer to mix everything until fluffy.
4. Pour into greased mugs.
5. Place the mugs in the fryer basket.
6. Bake for 15 minutes at 350°F.
7. Place in the fridge to chill before serving.

SHOPPING LIST

- ½ cup of cocoa powder
- ½ cup stevia powder
- 1 cup coconut cream
- 1 package cream cheese, room temperature
- 1 tablespoon vanilla extract
- 1 tablespoons butter

15 MINUTES

3

5 MINUTES

Angel Food Cake

INTERMEDIATE RECIPE

NUTRITION

Calories 65
Protein 3.1g
Fat 5g
Fiber 1g

SHOPPING LIST

- ¼ cup butter, melted
- 1 cup powdered erythritol
- 1 teaspoon strawberry extract
- 12 egg whites
- 2 teaspoons cream of tartar
- A pinch of salt

DIRECTIONS

1. Preheat the Cuisinart Air Fryer Oven for 5 minutes.
2. Mix the egg whites and cream of tartar.
3. Use a hand mixer and whisk until white and fluffy.
4. Add the rest of the ingredients except for the butter and whisk for another minute.
5. Pour into a baking dish.
6. Place in the air fryer basket and cook for 30 minutes at 400°F or if a toothpick inserted in the middle comes out clean.
7. Drizzle with melted butter once cooled.

5 MINUTES

30 MINUTES

12

Fried Peaches

BASIC RECIPE

NUTRITION

Calories 306   Protein 10g
Fat 3g   Fiber 2.7g

SHOPPING LIST

- 4 ripe peaches (1/2 a peach = 1 serving)
- 1 1/2 cups flour
- Salt
- 2 egg yolks
- 3/4 cups cold water
- 1 1/2 tablespoons olive oil
- 2 tablespoons brandy
- 4 egg whites
- Cinnamon/sugar mix

DIRECTIONS

1. Mix flour, egg yolks, and salt in a mixing bowl. Slowly mix in water, then add brandy.
2. Set the mixture aside for 2 hours and go do something for 1 hour 45 minutes.
3. Boil a large pot of water and cut and X at the bottom of each peach. While the water boils fill another large bowl with water and ice.
4. Boil each peach for about a minute, then plunge it in the ice bath. Now the peels should fall off the peach.
5. Beat the egg whites and mix into the batter mix.
6. Dip each peach in the mix to coat.
7. Pour the coated peach into the Oven rack/ basket. Place the Rack on the middle,shelf of the Cuisinart Air Fryer Oven.
8. Set temperature to 360°F, and set time to 10 minutes.
9. Prepare a plate with cinnamon/sugar mix, roll peaches in the mix and serve.

2H10 MINUTES

15 MINUTES

4

Apple Dumpling

INTERMEDIATE RECIPE

DIRECTIONS

1. Ensure your Cuisinart Air Fryer Oven is preheated to 356⁰F.
2. Core and peel apples and mix with raisins and sugar.
3. Place a bit of apple mixture into puff pastry sheets and brush sides with melted coconut oil.
4. Place into the air fryer. Cook 25 minutes, turning halfway through.
5. Will be golden when done.

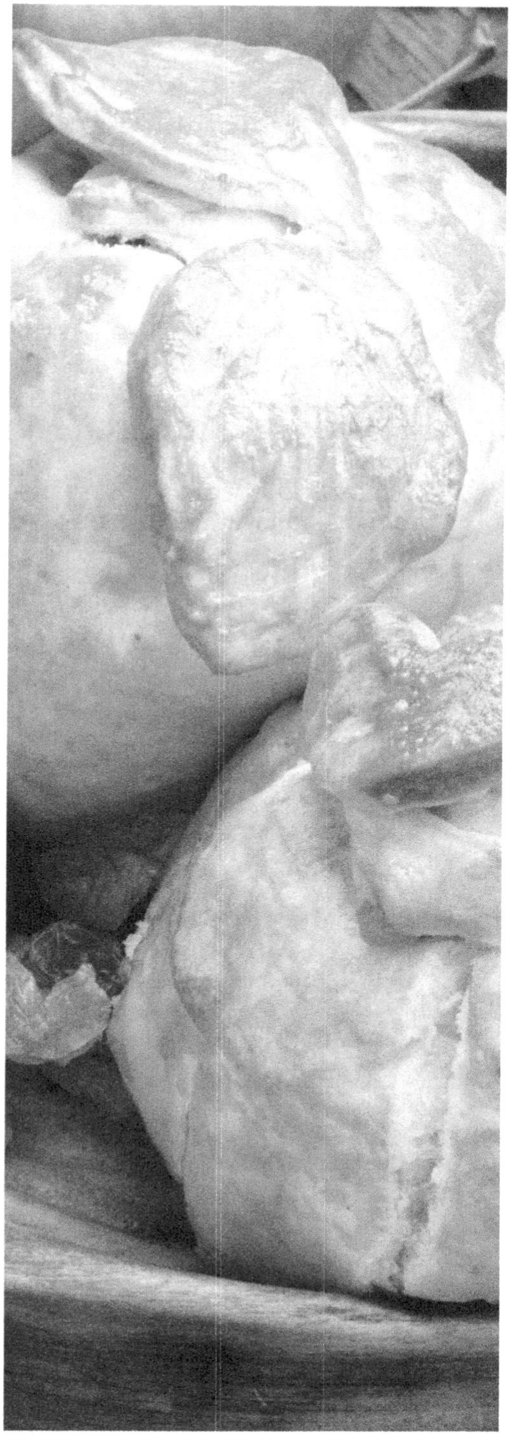

SHOPPING LIST

- 2 tablespoon melted coconut oil
- 2 puff pastry sheets
- 1 tablespoon brown sugar
- 2 tablespoon raisins
- 2 small apples of choice

NUTRITION

Calories 367
Fat 7g
Protein 2g
Sugar 5g

10 MINUTES

25 MINUTES

4

Apple Pie in Air Fryer

BASIC RECIPE

DIRECTIONS

1. Lightly grease baking pan of Cuisinart Air Fryer Oven with cooking spray.
2. Spread pie crust on the bottom of the pan up to the sides.
3. In a bowl, mix vanilla, sugar, cinnamon, lemon juice, and apples.
4. Pour on top of pie crust. Top apples with butter slices.
5. Cover apples with the other pie crust. Pierce with a knife the tops of the pie.
6. Spread beaten egg on top of crust and sprinkle sugar. Cover with foil.
7. For 25 minutes, cook on 390°F.
8. Remove foil cook for 10 minutes at 330°F until tops are browned. Serve and enjoy.

SHOPPING LIST

- ½ teaspoon vanilla extract
- 1 beaten egg
- 1 large apple, chopped
- 1 Pillsbury Refrigerator pie crust
- 1 tablespoon butter
- 1 tablespoon ground cinnamon
- 1 tablespoon raw sugar
- 2 tablespoon sugar
- 2 teaspoons lemon juice
- Baking spray

NUTRITION

Calories 372	Protein 4.2g
Fat 19g	Sugar 5g

5 MINUTES

35 MINUTES

4

Raspberry Cream Roll-Ups

NTERMEDIATE RECIPE

NUTRITION

Calories 412 Protein 5.2g
Fat 22g Sugar 7g

SHOPPING LIST

- For the Dough
- 1/2 tablespoon instant yeast
- 1/2 cup warm milk
- 3 tablespoons sugar
- 1/4 cup butter, well softened, but not melted
- 1/2 teaspoon salt
- 1 egg
- 2 cups all-purpose flour
- For the Cream Cheese Filling
- 4 ounces cream cheese, softened
- 2 tablespoons butter, softened
- 1/4 cup granulated sugar
- 1 teaspoon vanilla
- For the Raspberry Filling
- 1 and 1/2 cups frozen raspberries
- 1/2 tablespoon cornstarch

DIRECTIONS

1. Cover the basket of the Cuisinart Air Fryer Oven with a lining of tin foil, leaving the edges uncovered to allow air to circulate through the basket. Preheat the Cuisinart Air Fryer Oven to 350°F.
2. In a mixing bowl, combine the cream cheese, brown sugar, condensed milk, cornstarch, and egg. Beat or whip thoroughly, until all ingredients are completely mixed and fluffy, thick and stiff.
3. Spoon even amounts of the creamy filling into each spring roll wrapper, then top each dollop of filling with several raspberries.
4. Roll up the wraps around the creamy raspberry filling, and seal the seams with a few dabs of water.
5. Place each roll on the foil-lined air fryer basket, seams facing down.
6. Set the Cuisinart Air Fryer Oven timer to 10 minutes. During cooking, shake the handle of the fryer basket to ensure a nice even surface crisp.
7. After 10 minutes, when the Cuisinart Air Fryer Oven shuts off, the spring rolls should be golden brown and perfect on the outside, while the raspberries and cream filling will have cooked together in a glorious fusion.
8. Remove with tongs and serve hot or cold

10 MINUTES

25 MINUTES

4

Air Fryer Chocolate Cake

INTERMEDIATE RECIPES

NUTRITION

Calories 378 Protein 4g
Fat 9g Sugar 5g

DIRECTIONS

5 MINUTES

35 MINUTES

8-10

SHOPPING LIST

- ½ C. hot water
- 1 teaspoon vanilla
- ¼ cup olive oil
- ½ cup almond milk
- 1 egg
- ½ teaspoon salt
- ¾ teaspoon baking soda
- ¾ teaspoon baking powder
- ½ cup unsweetened cocoa powder
- 2 cup almond flour
- 1 cup brown sugar

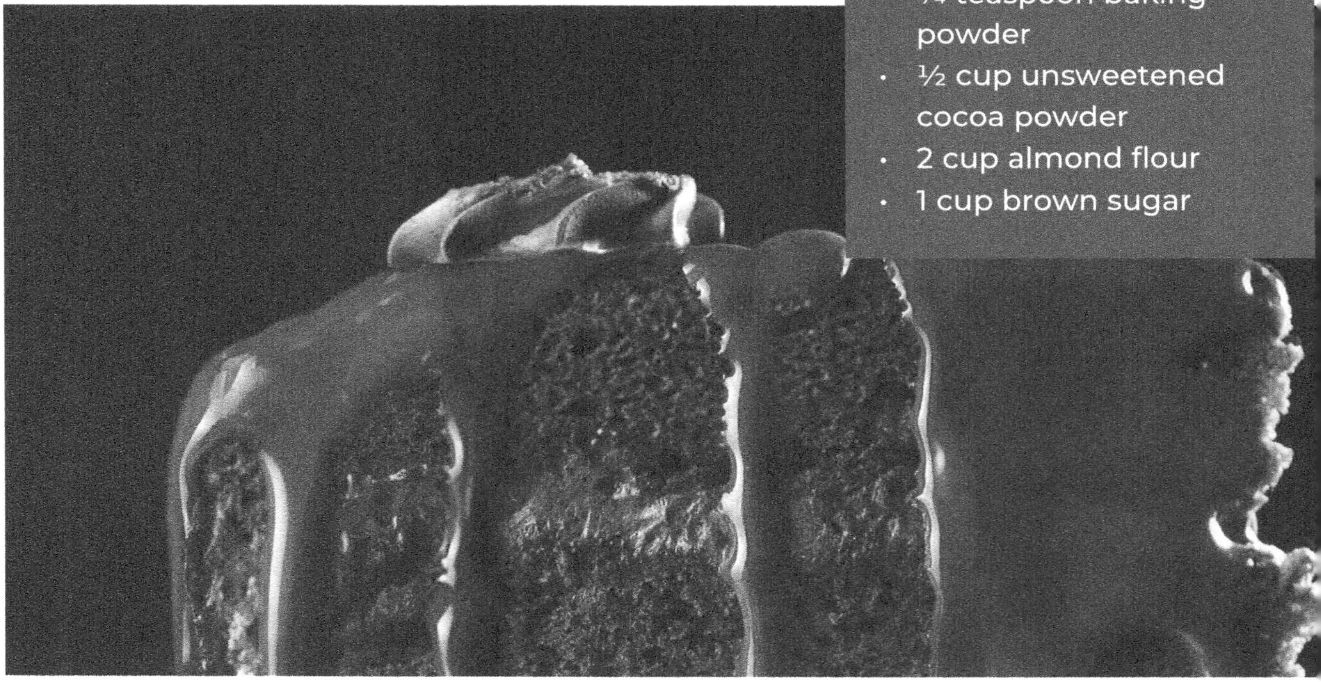

Banana-Choco Brownies

INTERMEDIATE RECIPE

12

5 MINUTES

30 MINUTES

NUTRITION

Calories 75 | Protein 1.7g
Fat 6.5g | Sugar 2g

SHOPPING LIST

- 2 cups almond flour
- 2 teaspoons baking powder
- ½ teaspoon baking powder
- ½ teaspoon baking soda
- ½ teaspoon salt
- 1 over-ripe banana
- 3 large eggs
- ½ teaspoon stevia powder
- ¼ cup of coconut oil
- 1 tablespoon vinegar
- 1/3 cup almond flour
- 1/3 cup cocoa powder

DIRECTIONS

1. Preheat the Cuisinart Air Fryer Oven for 5 minutes.
2. Combine all ingredients in a food processor and pulse until well-combined.
3. Pour into a baking dish that will fit in the air fryer.
4. Place in the air fryer basket and cook for 30 minutes at 350°F or if a toothpick inserted in the middle comes out clean.

Chocolate Donuts

BASIC RECIPE

NUTRITION

Calories 181
Protein 3g
Fat 98g
Fiber 1g

SHOPPING LIST

- (8-ounce) can jumbo biscuits
- Cooking oil
- Chocolate sauce, such as Hershey's

DIRECTIONS

1. Separate the biscuit dough into 8 biscuits and place them on a flat work surface. Use a small circle cookie cutter or a biscuit cutter to cut a hole in the center of each biscuit.
2. You can also cut the holes using a knife.
3. Spray the air fryer basket with cooking oil.
4. Place 4 donuts in the Cuisinart Air Fryer
5. Oven. Do not stack. Spray with cooking oil.
6. Cook for 4 minutes.
7. Open the air fryer and flip the donuts. Cook for an additional 4 minutes.
8. Remove the cooked donuts from the
9. Cuisinart Air Fryer Oven, then repeat for the remaining 4 donuts.
10. Drizzle chocolate sauce over the donuts and enjoy while warm.

5 MINUTES

20 MINUTES

8-10

Easy Air Fryer Donuts

BASIC RECIPE

SHOPPING LIST

- Pinch of allspice
- 4 tablespoons dark brown sugar
- ½ - 1 teaspoon cinnamon
- 1/3 C. granulated sweetener
- 3 tablespoon melted coconut oil
- 1 can of biscuits

NUTRITION

Calories 209
Fat 4g
Protein 0g
Sugar 3g

DIRECTIONS

1. Mix all spice, sugar, sweetener, and cinnamon.
2. Take out biscuits from the can and with a cookie circle cutter, cut holes from centers and place into the air fryer.
3. Cook 5 minutes at 350 degrees. As batches are cooked, use a brush to coat with melted coconut oil and dip each into a sugar mixture.
4. Serve warm!

Chocolate Soufflé for Two

INTERMEDIATE RECIPE

SHOPPING LIST

- 2 tablespoon almond flour
- ½ teaspoon vanilla
- 3 tablespoon sweetener
- 2 separated eggs
- ¼ C. melted coconut oil
- 3 ounces of semi-sweet chocolate, chopped

DIRECTIONS

1. Brush coconut oil and sweetener onto ramekins.
2. Melt coconut oil and chocolate together.
3. Beat egg yolks well, adding vanilla and sweetener. Stir in flour and ensure there are no lumps.
4. Preheat the Cuisinart Air Fryer Oven to 330°F.
5. Whisk egg whites till they reach peak state and fold them into chocolate mixture.
6. Pour batter into ramekins and place into the Cuisinart Air Fryer Oven. Cook 14 minutes.
7. Serve with powdered sugar dusted on top.

NUTRITION

Calories 238
Fat 6g
Protein 1g
Sugar 4g

5 MINUTES
14 MINUTES
2

Air Fryer Cajun Shrimp

BASIC RECIPE

NUTRITION

Calories 284
Carbohydrates 8g
Cholesterol 205mg
Protein 31g
fat 14g
Fiber 0.5 g
Sugar 0.5 g
Protein 7.1 g

DIRECTIONS

1. Place Cajun seasoning and shrimp in a large bowl and toss to mix
2. Add sausage, zucchini, bell peppers, yellow squash, salt and olive oil and toss
3. Preheat the fryer up to 400°F. Transfer the mix of shrimp and vegetables to air fryer and cook for 3 minutes; shake the basket intermittently during this time.
4. Repeat until all batches are done and then return the first batch to the oven and cook for 1 minute.

SHOPPING LIST

- 24 cleaned and peeled extra-jumbo shrimp (1
- pound)
- 2 tablespoon olive oil
- 1 medium yellow squash,
- (Slice into ¼ inch thick half-moon shape)
- 1 tablespoon Cajun seasoning
- ¼ tablespoon kosher salt
- 6 ounces fully cooked turkey or chicken
- Andouille sausage
- 1 large red bell pepper (remove seed and cut
- into 1 inch piece)
- 1 medium size zucchini, 8 ounces (slice int0
- ¼ inch half-moon shape)

10 MINUTES

20 MINUTES

4

Cacio E Pepe Air Fried Ravioli

INTERMEDIATE RECIPE

NUTRITION

Calories 655

Fat 28g

Sodium 1206mg

Fiber 3g

DIRECTIONS

1. Cook ravioli for 6 minutes in a pot of boiling water, after boiling, drain and set on paper towels to dry
2. Add breadcrumbs, 1/3 cups of pecorino, 1 teaspoon of black pepper, 1/3 cup of Parmigiano reggiano in a dish and mix .
3. Get another dish and place eggs in it.
4. Dip ravioli in egg then coat in bread crumb mixture (coat both sides properly).
5. Arrange ravioli into air fryer baskets in batches and coat lightly with cooking spray.
6. Set air fryer at 350⁰F for 7 minutes (turn halfway)
7. When ravioli is done, sprinkle cheese, pepper and parsley
8. Serve with marinara (optional)

SHOPPING LIST

- 1 cup Italian season breadcrumbs
- 3 large eggs (largely beaten)
- 1 kg refrigerated ravioli
- 1 tablespoon chopped fresh flat-leaf parsley
- 1/3 cup Pecorino romano cheese
- 1 1/3 teaspoon Black pepper, divided
- Warm marinara sauce, optional
- 1/3 cup Parmigiano reggiano cheese

15 MINUTES

10

5 MINUTES

Oats Sandwich Biscuits

BASIC RECIPE

NUTRITION

Calories 389 | Saturated Fat 11g | Sodium 103mg
Total Fat 14g | Cholesterol 37mg | Total Carbohydrates 54g

DIRECTIONS

1. Whisk butter with Sugar in an electric mixer until fluffy. Stir in egg, vanilla essence, coconut, and chocolate then mix well.
2. Slow add flour and continue mixing until it forms a cookie dough. Make medium-sized biscuits out of it then roll them in the oats to coat.
3. Place the cookies in the air fryer basket.
4. Cook the cookies in batches to avoid overcrowding. Set the air fryer basket in the instant pot duo. Put on the air fryer lid and seal it.
5. Hit the "air fry button" and select 18 minutes of Cooking time, then press "start."
6. Flip the cookies after 9 minutes then resume Cooking. Once the instant pot duo beeps, remove its lid.
7. Air fry the remaining cookies in the same manner.
8. Meanwhile, beat butter with icing Sugar into the creamy mixture. Stir in vanilla and lemon juice, then mix well.
9. Spread a tablespoon of this filling in between two cookies and make a sandwich out of them.
10. Use the entire filling to make more cookie sandwiches. Serve.

SHOPPING LIST

- 1 ½ cups plain flour
- 5 oz. Butter
- 3 oz. White Sugar
- ½ small egg beaten
- ¼ cup desiccated coconut
- ½ cup gluten-free oats
- 1/3 oz. White chocolate
- 1 teaspoon vanilla essence
- Filling:
- 5 oz. Icing Sugar
- 2 oz. Butter
- 1/2 teaspoon lemon juice
- 1 teaspoon vanilla essence

10 MINUTES

18 MINUTES

6

Chocolate Smarties Cookies

BASIC RECIPE

NUTRITION

Calories 372
Total Fat 16g
Saturated Fat 8g
Cholesterol 38mg
Sodium 108mg
Total Carbohydrates 53g

SHOPPING LIST

- 5 oz. Butter
- 5 oz. Caster Sugar
- 8 oz. Self-rising flour
- 1 teaspoon vanilla essence
- 5 tablespoon milk
- 3 tablespoon cocoa powder
- 2 oz. Nestle smarties

DIRECTIONS

1. Whisk cocoa powder with caster Sugar and self-rising flour in a bowl.
2. Stir in butter and mix well to form a crumbly mixture.
3. Stir in milk and vanilla essence, then mix well to form a smooth dough.
4. Add the smarties and knead the dough well.
5. Roll this cookie dough into a 1-inch thick layer. Use a cookies cutter to cut maximum cookies out of it.
6. Roll the remaining dough again to carve out more cookies.
7. Place half of the cookies in the air fryer basket. Set the air fryer basket in the instant pot duo.
8. Put on the air fryer lid and seal it.
9. Hit the "bake" button and select 10 minutes of Cooking time, then press "start." Flip the cookies after 5 minutes then resume Cooking.
10. Once the instant pot duo beeps, remove its lid.
11. similarly bake the remaining cookies.

Enjoy!

Pumpkin Cookies

BASIC RECIPE

DIRECTIONS

1. In a bowl, mix flax seed with water, stir and leave aside for a few minutes.
2. In another bowl, mix flour with salt and baking soda.
3. In a third bowl, mix honey with pumpkin puree, butter, vanilla extract and flaxseed.
4. Combine flour with honey mix and chocolate chips and stir.
5. Scoop 1 tablespoon of cookie dough on a lined baking sheet that fits your air fryer, repeat with the rest of the dough, introduce them in your air fryer and cook at 350°F for 15 minutes.
6. Leave cookies to cool down and serve.

SHOPPING LIST

- 2 and ½ cups flour
- ½ teaspoon baking soda
- 1 tablespoon flax seed, ground
- 3 tablespoons water
- ½ cup pumpkin flesh, mashed
- ¼ cup honey
- 2 tablespoons butter
- 1 teaspoon vanilla extract
- ½ cup dark chocolate chips

NUTRITION

Calories 140
Fat 2
Fiber 2
Carbs7
Protein 10

10 MINUTES

15 MINUTES

24

Figs and Coconut Butter Mix

INTERMEDIATE RECIPE

NUTRITION

Calories 170 Fiber 5 Protein 9
Fat 4 Carbs7

SHOPPING LIST

- 2 tablespoons coconut butter
- 12 figs, halved
- ¼ cup Sugar
- 1 cup almonds, toasted and chopped

DIRECTIONS

1. Put butter in a pan that fits your air fryer and melt over medium-high heat.
2. Add figs, Sugar and almonds, toss, introduce in your air fryer and cook at 300°F for 4 minutes.
3. Divide into bowls and serve cold.
4. Enjoy!

6 MINUTES

4 MINUTES

3

Sweet Squares

BASIC RECIPES

10 MINUTES

30 MINUTES

6

NUTRITION

Calories 100 Fiber 1 Protein 1

Fat 4 Carbs12

SHOPPING LIST

- 1 cup flour
- ½ cup butter, soft
- 1 cup Sugar
- ¼ cup powdered Sugar
- 2 teaspoons lemon peel, grated
- 2 tablespoons lemon juice
- 2 eggs, whisked
- ½ teaspoon baking powder

DIRECTIONS

1. In a bowl, mix flour with powdered Sugar and butter, stir well, press on the bottom of a pan that fits your air fryer, introduce in the fryer and bake at 350°F for 14 minutes.
2. In another bowl, mix Sugar with lemon juice, lemon peel, eggs and baking powder, stir using your mixer and spread over baked crust.
3. Bake for 15 minutes more, leave aside to cool down, cut into medium squares and serve cold.
4. Enjoy!

Plum Bars

BASIC RECIPE

8

10
MINUTES

16
MINUTES

NUTRITION

Calories 111 Fiber 6 Protein 6
Fat 5 Carbs12

SHOPPING LIST

- 2 cups dried plums
- 6 tablespoons water
- 2 cup rolled oats
- 1 cup brown Sugar
- ½ teaspoon baking soda
- 1 teaspoon cinnamon powder
- 2 tablespoons butter, melted
- 1 egg, whisked
- Cooking oil for spraying

DIRECTIONS

1. In your food processor, mix plums with water and blend until you obtain a sticky spread.
2. In a bowl, mix oats with cinnamon, baking soda, Sugar, egg and butter and whisk well.
3. Press half of the oats mix in a baking pan that fits your air fryer sprayed with Cooking oil, spread plums mix and top with the other half of the oats mix.
4. Introduce in your air fryer and cook at 350°F for 16 minutes.
5. Leave mix aside to cool down, cut into medium bars and serve.
6. Enjoy!

Chocolate Soufflé

BASIC RECIPE

NUTRITION

Calories 591	Cholesterol 225 mg	Fiber 0.2 g
Total Fat 38.7 g	Sodium 225 mg	Sugar 41.1 g
Saturated Fat 23 g	Total Carbs 52.6 g	Protein 9.4 g

15 MINUTES

16 MINUTES

2

SHOPPING LIST

- 3 oz. semi-sweet chocolate, chopped
- ¼ cup butter
- 2 eggs, yolks and whites separated
- 3 tablespoons sugar
- ½ teaspoon pure vanilla extract
- 2 tablespoons all-purpose flour
- 1 teaspoon powdered sugar plus extra for dusting

DIRECTIONS

1. In a microwave-safe bowl, place the butter, and chocolate. Microwave on high heat for about 2 minutes or until melted completely, stirring after every 30 seconds.
2. Remove from the microwave and stir the mixture until smooth.
3. In another bowl, add the egg yolks and whisk well.
4. Add the sugar, and vanilla extract and whisk well.
5. Add the chocolate mixture and mix until well combined. Add the flour and mix well.
6. In a clean glass bowl, add the egg whites and whisk until soft peaks form.
7. Fold the whipped egg whites in 3 portions into the chocolate mixture.
8. Grease 2 ramekins and sprinkle each with a pinch of sugar.
9. Place mixture into the prepared 240 ramekins and with the back of a spoon, smooth the top surface.
10. Press the "Power Button" of the Air Fry Oven and turn the dial to select the "Air Fry" mode.
11. Press the Time button and again turn the dial to set the cooking time to 14 minutes.
12. Now push the Temp button and rotate the dial to set the temperature at 330°F.
13. Press the "Start/Pause" button to start.
14. When the unit beeps to show that it is preheated, open the lid.
15. Arrange the ramekins in "Air Fry Basket" and insert them in the oven.
16. Place the ramekins onto a wire rack to cool slightly.
17. Sprinkle with the powdered sugar and serve warm.

Fudge Brownies

BASIC RECIPE

SHOPPING LIST

- 1 cup of sugar
- ½ cup butter, melted
- ½ cup flour
- 1/3 cup cocoa powder
- 1 teaspoon baking powder
- 2 eggs
- 1 teaspoon vanilla extract

NUTRITION

Calories 250	Cholesterol 71 mg	Fiber 1.3 g
Total Fat 13.2 g	Sodium 99 mg	Sugar 25.2 g
Saturated Fat 7.9 g	Total Carbs 33.4 g	Protein 3 g

DIRECTIONS

1. Grease a baking pan.
2. In a large bowl, add the sugar, and butter and whisk until light and fluffy.
3. Add the remaining ingredients and mix until well combined.
4. Place mixture into the prepared pan and with the back of the spatula, smooth the top surface.
5. Press "Power Button" of Air Fry Oven and turn the dial to select the "Air Fry" mode.
6. Press the Time button and again turn the dial to set the cooking time to 20 minutes.
7. Now push the Temp button and rotate the dial to set the temperature at 350°F.
8. Press the "Start/ Pause" button to start.
9. When the unit beeps to show that it is preheated, open the lid.
10. Arrange the pan in "Air Fry Basket" and insert it in the oven.
11. Place the baking pan onto a wire rack to cool completely.
12. Cut into 8 equal-sized squares and serve.

Walnut Brownies

INTERMEDIATE RECIPE

SHOPPING LIST

- ½ cup chocolate, roughly chopped
- 1/3 cup butter
- 5 tablespoons sugar
- 1 egg, beaten
- 1 teaspoon vanilla extract
- Pinch of salt
- 5 tablespoons self-rising flour
- ¼ cup walnuts, chopped

DIRECTIONS

1. In a microwave-safe bowl, add the chocolate and butter. Microwave on high heat for about 2 minutes, stirring after every 30 seconds. Remove from microwave and set aside to cool.
2. In another bowl, add the sugar, egg, vanilla extract, and salt and whisk until creamy and light.
3. Add the chocolate mixture and whisk until well combined.
4. Add the flour, and walnuts and mix until well combined.
5. Line a baking pan with a greased parchment paper.
6. Place mixture evenly into the prepared pan and with the back of the spatula, smooth the top surface.
7. Press "Power Button" of Air Fry Oven and turn the dial to select the "Air Fry" mode.
8. Press the Time button and again turn the dial to set the cooking time to 20 minutes.
9. Now push the Temp button and rotate the dial to set the temperature at 355 degrees F.
10. Press the "Start/Pause" button to start. When the unit beeps to show that it is preheated, open the lid. Arrange the pan in "Air Fry Basket" and insert it in the oven.
11. Place the baking pan onto a wire rack to cool completely.
12. Cut into 4 equal-sized squares and serve.

15 MINUTES

22 MINUTES

4

NUTRITION

Calories 407
Total Fat 27.4g
Saturated Fat 14.7 g
Cholesterol 86 mg
Sodium 180 mg
Total Carbs 35.9 g
Fiber 1.5 g
Sugar 26.2 g
Protein 6 g

Plum and Currant Tart

BASIC RECIPE

NUTRITION

Calories 200
Fat 5
Fiber 4
Carbs 8
Protein 6

DIRECTIONS

1. In a bowl, mix brown rice flour with ½ cup
2. Sugar, millet flour, almond flour, butter and milk and stir until you obtain sand-like dough.
3. Reserve ¼ of the dough, press the rest of the dough into a tart pan that fits your air fryer and keeps it in the fridge for 30 minutes.
4. Meanwhile, in a bowl, mix plums with currants, 3 tablespoons Sugar, cornstarch, vanilla extract, cinnamon, ginger and lime juice and stir well. Pour this over tart crust, crumble reserved dough on top, introduce in your air fryer and cook at 350°F for 35 minutes.
5. Leave the tart to cool down, slice and serve.
6. Enjoy!

SHOPPING LIST

- For the crumble:
- ¼ cup almond flour
- ¼ cup millet flour
- 1 cup brown rice flour
- ½ cup cane Sugar
- 10 tablespoons butter, soft
- 3 tablespoons milk
- For the filling:
- 1-pound small plums, pitted and halved
- 1 cup white currants
- 2 tablespoons cornstarch
- 3 tablespoons Sugar
- ½ teaspoon vanilla extract
- ½ teaspoon cinnamon powder
- ¼ teaspoon ginger powder
- 1 teaspoon lime juice

30 MINUTES

35 MINUTES

6

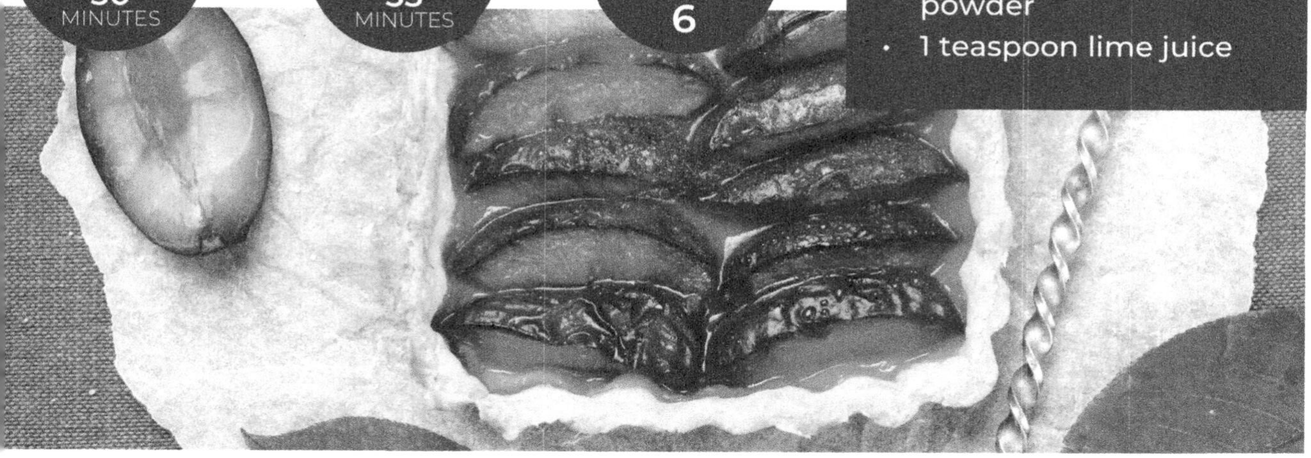

Tasty Orange Cookies

BASIC RECIPE

NUTRITION

Calories 124 | Fiber 6 | Protein 4
Fat 5 | Carbs8

DIRECTIONS

1. In a bowl, mix cream cheese with ½ cup butter and 2 cups powdered Sugar, stir well using your mixer and leave aside for now.
2. In another bowl, mix flour with baking powder.
3. In a third bowl, mix ½ cup butter with ¾ cup Sugar, egg, vanilla extract and orange zest and whisk well.
4. Combine flour with an orange mix, stir well and scoop 1 tablespoon of the mix on a lined baking sheet that fits your air fryer.
5. Repeat with the rest of the orange batter, introduce in the fryer and cook at 340°F for 12 minutes.
6. Leave cookies to cool down, spread cream filling on half of the top with the other cookies and serve. Enjoy!

SHOPPING LIST

- 2 cups flour
- 1 teaspoon baking powder
- ½ cup butter, soft
- ¾ cup Sugar
- 1 egg, whisked
- 1 teaspoon vanilla extract
- 1 tablespoon orange zest, grated
- For the filling:
- 4 ounces cream cheese, soft
- ½ cup butter
- 2 cups powdered Suga

12 MINUTES

8

10 MINUTES

Cashew Bars

BASIC RECIPE

10 MINUTES

15 MINUTES

6

NUTRITION

Calories 121 Fiber 7 Protein 6
Fat 4 Carbs5

DIRECTIONS

1. In a bowl, mix honey with almond meal and almond butter and stir well.
2. Add cashews, coconut, dates and chia seeds and stir well again.
3. Spread this on a lined baking sheet that fits your air fryer and press well.
4. Introduce in the fryer and cook at 300°F for 15 minutes.
5. Leave the mix to cool down, cut into medium bars, and serve.
6. Enjoy!

SHOPPING LIST

- 1/3 cup honey
- ¼ cup almond meal
- 1 tablespoon almond butter
- 1 and ½ cups cashews, chopped
- 4 dates, chopped
- ¾ cup coconut, shredded
- 1 tablespoon chia seeds

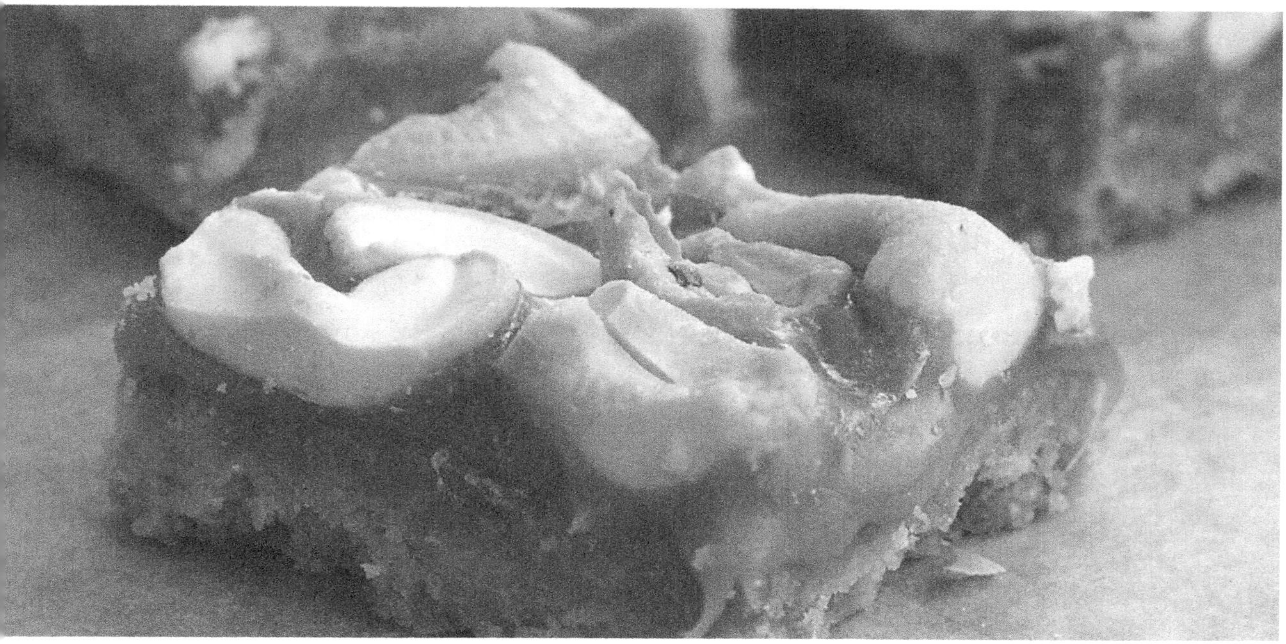

Brown Butter Cookies

BASIC RECIPE

NUTRITION

Calories 144
Fat 5
Fiber 6
Carbs19
Protein 2

SHOPPING LIST

- 1 and ½ cups butter
- 2 cups brown Sugar
- 2 eggs, whisked
- 3 cups flour
- 2/3 cup pecans, chopped
- 2 teaspoons vanilla extract
- 1 teaspoon baking soda
- ½ teaspoon baking powder

DIRECTIONS

1. Heat a pan with the butter over medium heat, stir until it melts, add brown Sugar and stir until these dissolve.
2. In a bowl, mix flour with pecans, vanilla extract, baking soda, baking powder and eggs and stir well.
3. Add brown butter, stir well and arrange a spoonful of this mix on a lined baking sheet that fits your air fryer.
4. Introduce in the fryer and cook at 340°F for 10 minutes.
5. Leave cookies to cool down and serve.
6. Enjoy!

10 MINUTES

10 MINUTES

6

Sweet Potato Cheesecake

BASIC RECIPE

DIRECTIONS

1. In a bowl, mix butter with crumbled crackers, stir well, press on the bottom of a cake pan that fits your air fryer and keep in the fridge for now.
2. In another bowl, mix cream cheese with mascarpone, sweet potato puree, milk, cinnamon and vanilla and whisk well.
3. Spread this over crust, introduce in your air fryer, cook at 300⁰F for 4 minutes and keep in the fridge for a few hours before serving.
4. Enjoy!

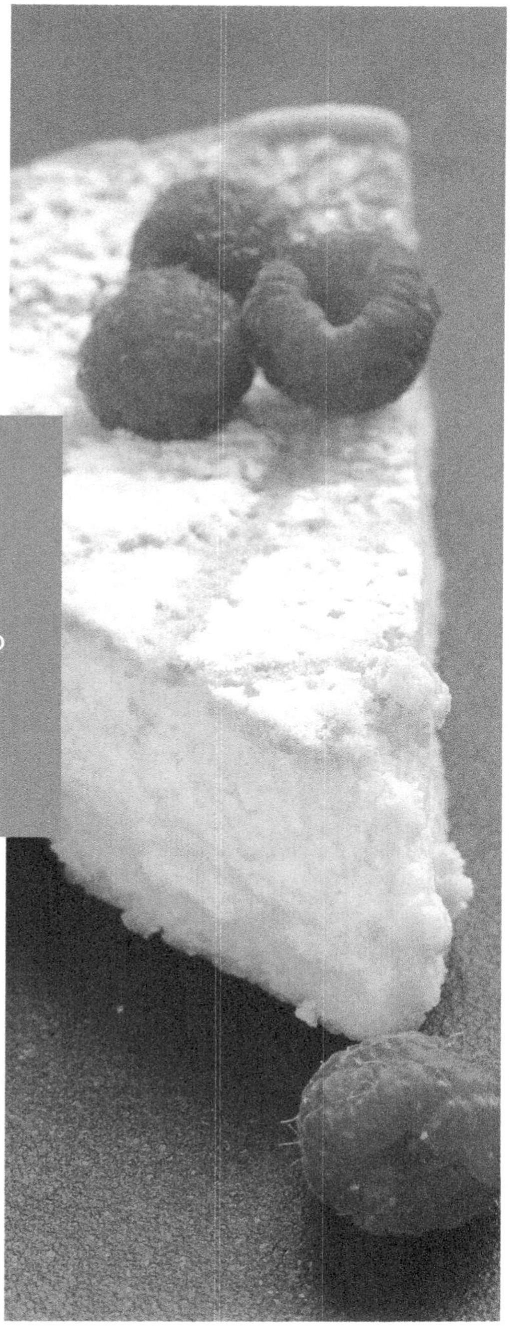

SHOPPING LIST

- 4 tablespoons butter, melted
- 6 ounces mascarpone, soft
- 8 ounces cream cheese, soft
- 2/3 cup graham crackers, crumbled
- ¾ cup milk
- 1 teaspoon vanilla extract
- 2/3 cup sweet potato puree
- ¼ teaspoons cinnamon powder

NUTRITION

Calories 172
Fat 4
Fiber 6
Carbs8
Protein 3

10 MINUTES

5 MINUTES

4

Peach Pie

BASIC RECIPE

NUTRITION

Calories 231 | Fiber 7 | Protein 5
Fat 6 | Carbs 9

SHOPPING LIST

- 1 pie dough
- 2 and ¼ pounds peaches, pitted and
- chopped
- 2 tablespoons cornstarch
- ½ cup Sugar
- 2 tablespoons flour
- A pinch of nutmeg, ground
- 1 tablespoon dark rum
- 1 tablespoon lemon juice
- 2 tablespoons butter, melted

DIRECTIONS

1. Roll pie dough into a pie pan that fits your air fryer and press well.
2. In a bowl, mix peaches with cornstarch, Sugar, flour, nutmeg, rum, lemon juice and butter and stir well.
3. Pour and spread this into a pie pan, introduce in your air fryer and cook at 350°F for 35 minutes.
4. Serve warm or cold.
5. Enjoy!

10 MINUTES

35 MINUTES

4

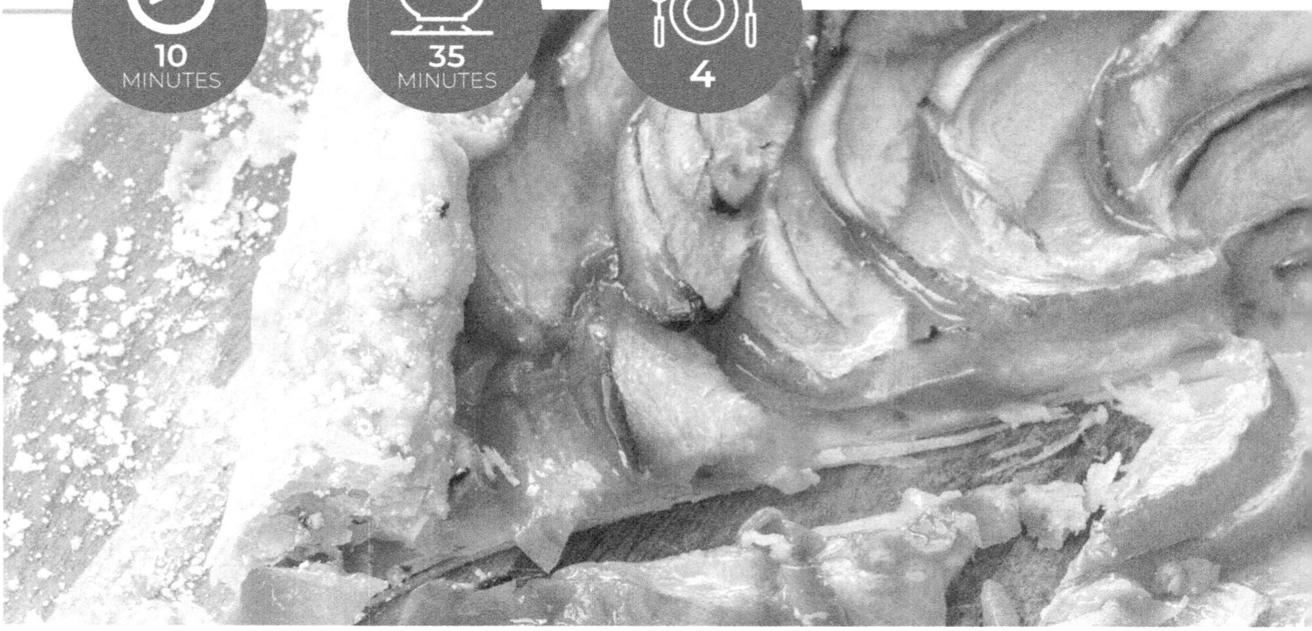

Chocolate Yogurt Muffins

INTERMEDIATE RECIPE

15 MINUTES

10 MINUTES

9

NUTRITION

Calories 246 | Protein 5g | Sugar 10.2g

Carbs 27.3g | Fat 12.9g | Sodium 159mg

SHOPPING LIST

- 1½ cups all-purpose flour
- ¼ cup of sugar
- 2 teaspoons baking powder
- ½ teaspoon salt
- 1 cup yogurt
- 1/3 cup vegetable oil
- 1 egg
- 2 teaspoons vanilla extract
- ¼ cup mini chocolate chips
- ¼ cup pecans, chopped

DIRECTIONS

1. In a bowl, mix well flour, sugar, baking powder, and salt.
2. In another bowl, add the yogurt, oil, egg, and vanilla extract and whisk until well combined.
3. Add the flour mixture and mix until just combined.
4. Fold in the chocolate chips and pecans.
5. Set the temperature of the air fryer to 355°F. Grease 9 muffin molds.
6. Place mixture evenly into the prepared muffin molds.
7. Arrange the muffin molds into an air fryer basket.
8. Air fry for 10 minutes or until a toothpick inserted in the center comes out clean.
9. Remove the muffin molds from the air fryer and place them onto a wire rack to cool for about 10 minutes.
10. Finally, invert the muffins onto a wire rack to completely cool before serving.

Brownies Muffins

BASIC RECIPE

12

10 MINUTES

16 MINUTES

NUTRITION

Calories 241 | Protein 2.8g | Sugar 25g
Carbs 36.9g | Fat 9.6g | Sodium 155mg

SHOPPING LIST

- 1 package Betty Crocker fudge brownie mix
- ¼ cup walnuts, chopped
- 1 egg
- 1/3 cup vegetable oil
- 2 teaspoons water

DIRECTIONS

1. In a bowl, mix well all the ingredients.
2. Set the temperature of the air fryer to 300°F.
3. Grease 12 muffin molds.
4. Place mixture evenly into the prepared muffin molds.
5. Arrange the molds into an Air Fryer basket.
   Air fry for 10 minutes or until a toothpick inserted in the center comes out clean.
6. Remove the muffin molds from the air fryer and place them onto a wire rack to cool for about 10 minutes.
7. Finally, invert the muffins onto a wire rack to completely cool before serving.

Double Chocolate Muffins

BASIC RECIPE

20 MINUTES

30 MINUTES

12

NUTRITION

Calories 207
Carbs 28.1g
Protein 3.3g
Fat 9.6g
Sugar 16.5g
Sodium 66mg

SHOPPING LIST

- 1 1/3 cups self-rising flour
- 2/3 cup plus 3 tablespoons caster sugar
- 2½ tablespoons cocoa powder
- 3½ ounces butter
- 5 tablespoons milk
- 2 medium eggs
- ½ teaspoon vanilla extract
- Water, as required
- 2½ ounces milk chocolate, finely chopped

DIRECTIONS

1. In a bowl, mix well flour, sugar, and cocoa powder.
2. With a pastry cutter, cut in the butter until a breadcrumb like mixture forms.
3. In another bowl, mix the milk, and eggs.
4. Add the egg mixture into the flour mixture and mix until well combined.
5. Add the vanilla extract and a little water and mix until well combined.
6. Fold in the chopped chocolate.
7. Set the temperature of the air fryer to 355°F. Grease 12 muffin molds.
8. Transfer mixture evenly into the prepared muffin molds.
9. Arrange the molds into an air fryer basket in 2 batches.
10. Air fry for about 9 minutes.
11. Now, set the temperature of the air fryer to 320°F.
12. Air fry for another 6 minutes or until a toothpick inserted in the center comes out clean.
13. Remove the muffin molds from the air fryer and place them onto a wire rack to cool for about 10 minutes.
14. Now, invert the muffins onto a wire rack to cool completely before serving.

Fruity Oreo Muffin

BASIC RECIPE

SHOPPING LIST

- 1 cup milk
- 1 pack Oreo biscuits, crushed
- 1 teaspoon of cocoa powder
- ¼ teaspoon baking soda
- ½ teaspoon baking powder
- 1 banana, peeled and chopped
- 1 apple, peeled, cored and chopped
- 1 teaspoon honey
- 1 teaspoon fresh lemon juice
- A pinch of ground cinnamon

NUTRITION

Calories 182
Carbs 31.4g
Protein 3.1g
Fat 5.9g
Sugar 19.5g
Sodium 196mg

DIRECTIONS

1. In a bowl, add the milk, biscuits, cocoa powder, baking soda, and baking powder.
2. Mix until a smooth mixture forms.
3. Set the temperature of the air fryer to 320°F. Grease 6 muffin cups.
4. Place mixture evenly into the prepared muffin cups.
5. Arrange the muffin cups into an air fryer basket.
6. Air fry for 10 minutes or until a toothpick inserted in the center comes out clean.
7. Remove from air fryer and place the muffin cups onto a wire rack to cool slightly.
8. Meanwhile, in another bowl, mix the banana, apple, honey, lemon juice, and cinnamon.
9. Carefully, scoop some portion of muffins from the center to make a cup.
10. Fill each cup with a fruit mixture.
11. Refrigerate to chill before serving.

15 MINUTES

10 MINUTES

6

Strawberry Cupcakes

BASIC RECIPE

SHOPPING LIST

- For Cupcakes
- ½ cup caster sugar
- 7 tablespoons butter
- 2 eggs
- ½ teaspoon vanilla essence
- 7/8 cup self-rising flour
- For Frosting
- 1 cup icing sugar
- 3½ tablespoons butter
- 1 tablespoon whipped cream
- ¼ cup fresh strawberries, pureed
- ½ teaspoon pink food color

DIRECTIONS

1. In a bowl, add butter, and sugar and whisk until fluffy and light.
2. Then, add the eggs, one at a time, and whisk until well combined.
3. Stir in the vanilla extract.
4. Gradually, add the flour whisking continuously until well combined.
5. Place the mixture into silicon cups.
6. Set the temperature of the air fryer to 340°F.
7. Arrange the silicon cups into an air fryer basket.
8. Air fry for about 8 minutes or until a toothpick inserted in the center comes out clean.
9. Remove the silicone cups from the air fryer and place them onto a wire rack to cool for about 10 minutes.
10. Now, invert the cupcakes onto a wire rack to completely cool before frosting.
11. For the frosting: in another bowl, add the icing sugar, and butter and whisk until fluffy and light. Add the whipped cream, strawberry puree, and color. Mix until well combined.
12. Fill the pastry bag with icing and decorate the cupcakes.

20 MINUTES

8 MINUTES

10

NUTRITION

Calories 250
Carbs 30.7g
Protein 2.4g
Fat 13.6g
Sugar 22.1g
Sodium 99mg

Raspberry Cupcakes

INTERMEDIATE RECIPE

NUTRITION

Calories 209
Fat 12.5g
Carbs 22.8g
Sugar 12.5g
Protein 2.7g
Sodium 110mg

DIRECTIONS

1. In a bowl, mix well flour, baking powder, and salt.
2. In another bowl, mix the cream cheese, and butter.
3. Add the sugar and whisk until fluffy and light.
4. Now, place the eggs, one at a time and whisk until just combined.
5. Add the flour mixture and stir until well combined.
6. Stir in the lemon juice.
7. Place the mixture evenly into silicone cups and top each with 2 raspberries.
8. Set the temperature of the air fryer to 365°F.
9. Arrange the silicon cups into an air fryer basket.
10. Air fry for about 15 minutes or until a toothpick inserted in the center comes out clean.
11. Remove the silicone cups from the air fryer and place them onto a wire rack to cool for about 10 minutes.
12. Now, invert the cupcakes onto a wire rack to completely cool before serving

SHOPPING LIST

- 4½ ounces self-rising flour
- ½ teaspoon baking powder
- A pinch of salt
- ½ ounce cream cheese, softened
- 4¾ ounces butter, softened
- 4¼ ounces caster sugar
- 2 eggs
- 2 teaspoons fresh lemon juice
- ½ cup fresh raspberries

15 MINUTES

15 MINUTES

10

Red Velvet Cupcakes

INTERMEDIATE RECIPE

NUTRITION

Calories 599 Protein 9.3g Sugar 53.4g
Carbs 73.2g Fat 31.5g Sodium 308mg

DIRECTIONS

For cupcakes: in a bowl, put all the ingredients and with an electric whisker, whisk until well combined. Place the mixture into silicone cups.
Set the temperature of the air fryer to 340°F. Arrange the silicon cups into an air fryer basket.
Air fry for about 10-12 minutes or until a toothpick inserted in the center comes out clean.
Remove the silicone cups from the air fryer and place them onto a wire rack to cool for about 10 minutes.
Now, invert the cupcakes onto a wire rack to completely cool before frosting. For the frosting: In a large bowl, mix well butter, cream cheese, vanilla extract, and salt.
Add the powdered sugar, one cup at a time, whisking well after each addition. Spread frosting evenly over each cupcake. Garnish with raspberries and serve.

12 MINUTES

12

20 MINUTES

SHOPPING LIST

- For Cupcakes
- 2 cups refined flour
- ¾ cup icing sugar
- 2 teaspoons of beet powder
- 1 teaspoon of cocoa powder
- ¾ cup peanut butter
- 3 eggs
- For Frosting
- 1 cup butter
- 1 (8-ounces) package cream cheese, softened
- 2 teaspoons vanilla extract
- ¼ teaspoon salt
- 4½ cups powdered sugar
- For Garnishing
- ½ cup fresh raspberries

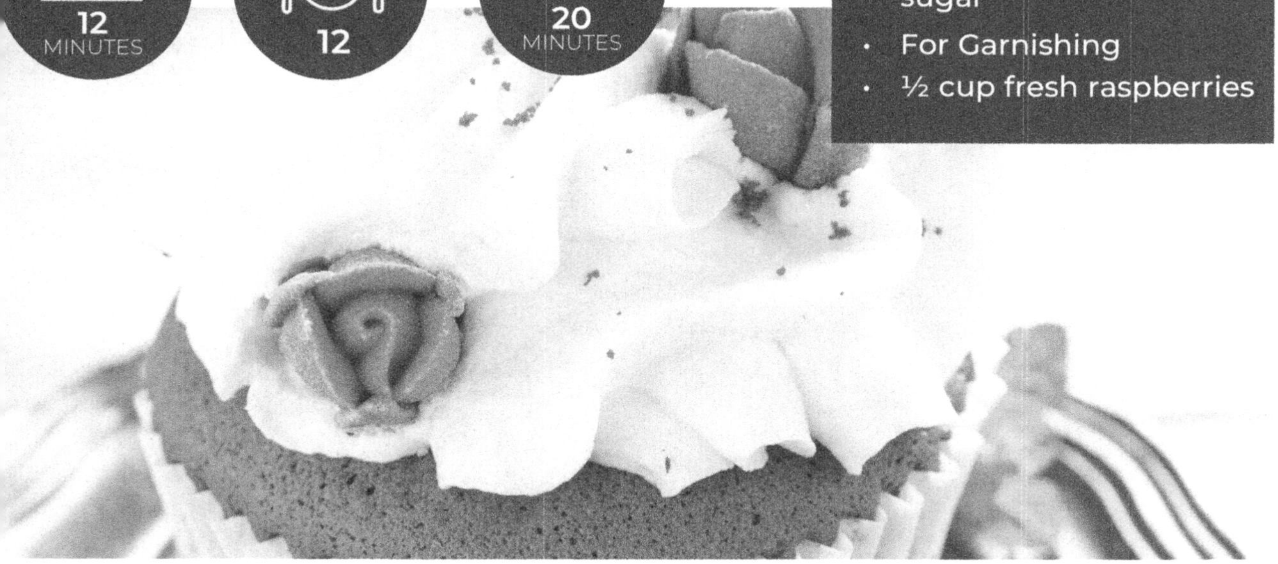

Semolina Cake

INTERMEDIATE RECIPE

NUTRITION

Calories 637 | Protein 13.9g | Sugar 41.7g
Carbs 94.8g | Fat 23.8g | Sodium 181mg

15 MINUTES

15 MINUTES

6

DIRECTIONS

1. In a bowl, mix well semolina, oil, milk, yogurt, and sugar. Cover and set aside for about 15 minutes.
2. Add the baking soda, baking powder, and salt in the bowl of semolina mixture and mix until well combined.
3. Fold in the raisins and walnuts. Set the temperature of the air fryer to 390°F grease a cake pan.
4. Place cake mixture evenly into the prepared cake pan. Arrange the cake pan into an air fryer basket. Now, set the temperature of the air fryer to 320°F. Air fry for about 15 minutes or until a toothpick inserted in the center comes out clean.
5. Remove the cake pan from the air fryer and place it onto a wire rack to cool for about 10 minutes. Now, invert the cake onto a wire rack. to completely cool before slicing.
6. Cut the cake into desired size slices and serve.

SHOPPING LIST

- 2½ cups semolina*
- ½ cup of vegetable oil
- 1 cup of milk
- 1 cup of plain Greek yogurt
- 1 cup of sugar
- ½ teaspoon baking soda
- 1½ teaspoons baking powder
- A pinch of salt
- ¼ cup raisins
- ¼ cup walnuts, chopped

Butter Cake

BASIC RECIPE

NUTRITION

Calories 291	Protein	Fat 12.9g	Sodium 129mg
Carbs 40.3g	4.6g	Sugar 19g	

DIRECTIONS

In a bowl, add the butter, and sugar and whisk until light and creamy. Add in the egg and whisk until smooth and fluffy. Now, add the flour, and salt and mix well alternately with the milk.

Set the temperature of the air fryer to 350°F
Grease a small Bundy cake pan.
Place mixture evenly into the prepared cake pan.
Arrange the cake pan in an air fryer basket.
Air fry for about 15 minutes or until a toothpick inserted into the center comes out clean.
Remove the cake pan from the air fryer and place it onto a wire rack to cool for about 10 minutes.
Now, invert the cake onto a wire rack to completely cool before slicing. Dust the cake with icing sugar and cut into desired size slices.

Serve!

SHOPPING LIST

- 3 ounces butter, softened
- ½ cup caster sugar
- 1 egg
- 1 1/3 cups plain flour, sifted
- A pinch of salt
- ½ cup milk
- 1 tablespoon icing

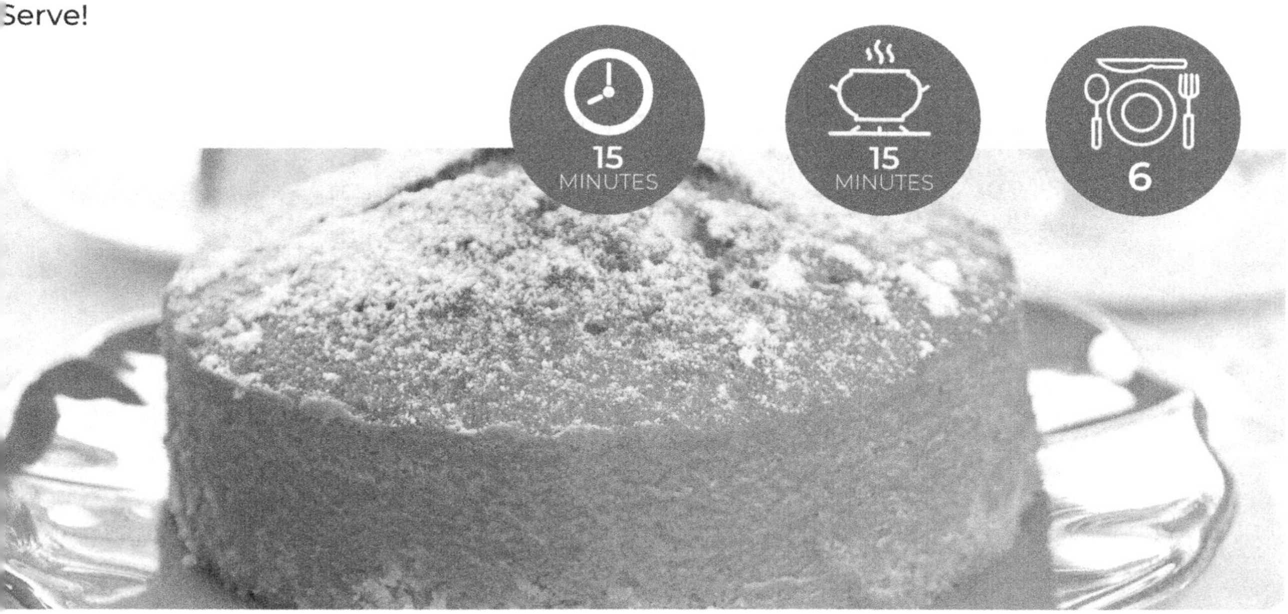

Conclusion

This is it! You have worked your way through this book. We hope that some of your misgivings about starting with your brand-new kitchen helper have been put to rest.

Remember, every person starts out being a beginner; we all have to learn what works best for us. Each time you make a new dish, you know more, and your experience grows.

Air fryers recreate the usual browning of foods by coursing hot air around food as opposed to submerging the food in oil. Similarly, as with searing, appropriately arranged foods are fresh, succulent, brilliant dark-colored, and delightful.

An air-fryer cooker or appliances is a convection oven in smaller than expected – a conservative round and hollow ledge convection oven, to be accurate (have a go at saying that multiple times quick).

This is truly the healthiest way to prepare food that everyone in the family will enjoy and keep coming back for more without them, even realizing that they are eating better.

Now you know everything you need to get started with your air fryer! Just pick a recipe to get started with low Sodium, low carb cooking in no time at all. Remember that healthy food doesn't mean that you need to slave away in the kitchen or pay big bucks for hand-delivered meals. All you need is to try new, delicious recipes that are sure to become family favorites in no time at all.

Your air fryer will soon be the most used item in your kitchen!

Recipes Index

N

O

P

Q

R

S

T

V

W

Y

Z

Made in United States
Orlando, FL
31 July 2022

20394926R00148